THE GAS GRILL GOURMET

THE
GAS GRILL
G·O·U·R·M·E·T

Great Grilled Food for Everyday Meals and Fantastic Feasts

A. CORT SINNES

with John Puscheck

◆ ◆ ◆

THE HARVARD COMMON PRESS
Boston, Massachusetts

THE HARVARD COMMON PRESS
535 Albany Street
Boston, Massachusetts 02118

Printed in the United States of America

Library of Congress Cataloging-in-Publication Data

Sinnes, A. Cort.
The gas grill gourmet: great grilled food for everyday meals and fantastic feasts / A. Cort
Sinnes, with John Puscheck.
p.   cm.
Includes index.
ISBN 1-55832-109-8. — ISBN 1-55832-110-1
1. Barbecue cookery. I. Puscheck, John. II. Title
TX840.B3S559 1996
641.5'784—dc20   96-22822

Special bulk-order discounts are available on this and other Harvard Common Press books.
Companies and organizations may purchase books for premiums or for resale,
or may arrange a custom edition, by contacting the Marketing Director at the address above.

Cover and text design by Kathleen Herlihy-Paoli, Inkstone Design
Illustrations by Chris Van Dusen
Cover photograph by Steven Needham/Envision

10   9   8   7   6   5   4   3   2   1

◆

To the Kindergarten Club.
It's hard to imagine better friends.

◆

CONTENTS

◆

ACKNOWLEDGMENTS

I am happy to thank the kind folks at several gas-grill manufacturers, for providing me with some wonderful cooking equipment; the Barbecue Industry Association, for facts about the history of gas grills and trends in their use; Rebecca Hanson and Amanda Bichsel at the Harvard Common Press, for help with innumerable details of the manuscript; John, Mark, and the gang at Ernie's Meat Market, for stocking the kind of food that makes cooking such a joy; Mike Landis, ace photographer, gourmand, and old friend; Tim, Tom, Jeanne, Patty, Mike, Deezie, Ruthie, Jennifer G., Jack, Michelle, and all the other late-night, drive-by taste testers; and Buster, who kept us entertained. Special thanks go to John Puscheck, a natural-born chef, whose culinary skills and knowledge always amaze.

INTRODUCTION

There's no doubt that gas grills are here to stay. Although it may be hard to believe, three-quarters of all American households own at least one barbecue grill. More than half of all households own a gas grill, and that number is growing every year. Americans love to grill.

Our grilling tastes are changing. Most of us continue to lust after a juicy hamburger or steak, but we are experimenters, too. Today we are grilling shellfish, game birds, vegetables, even fruit, and we are reveling in the new tastes and textures we can coax from our grills. The possibilities are astounding: grilled oysters, quesadillas, or stuffed grape leaves for starters; entrées of grilled lobster tails, beef saté, or portobello mushroom burgers, with sides of grilled ratatouille, leeks, or sweet potatoes; and grilled bananas or peaches, or even a dessert bruschetta, for the finale. Indeed, today's gourmet outdoor chef can prepare, with surprising ease, a superb four-course meal, stepping into the kitchen only briefly for some simple prep work. Grilling, that favorite American pastime, has grown up, and the results are delicious.

Grilling used to be seen as a summertime, weekend activity, but this is changing, too. The convenience of gas grills has contributed to a dramatic rise in year-round, weekday grilling for a great many households. Grilling gives us a respite from the kitchen, offering us a new kind of hearth around which to gather family and friends. Everyone enjoys the chance to relax a bit outdoors, to take a break from the routine, and, of course, to enjoy the honest-to-goodness flavor of grilled foods.

Gas grills have much to recommend them. They are extremely easy to light, easy to adjust to a variety of cooking temperatures, and clean-burning. Overall, gas grillers use their grills twice as often as charcoal grillers, and they are much more likely to use their grills throughout the year.

When the old charcoal grill finally burns out, most people today are choosing to replace it with a gas grill. Many of these people try to use the same cooking techniques they used on their charcoal grill on their new gas grill, often with less-than-successful results. The most important secret any gas grill cook should learn is indirect cooking—quite simply, grilling food out of the way of the direct heat source, a procedure described more fully later in this introduction. If you can break yourself of the habit of cooking directly over the heat, you will be amazed at how easy it is to grill foods that are succulent, juicy, and nicely browned, but definitely not burned.

For the record, gas grilling *is* different from charcoal cooking. Gas grills are easier to manage. They are cleaner-burning, resulting in what some people might call "cleaner-tasting" food, though still with a distinctive grilled flavor. In general, gas grills provide lower cooking temperatures than charcoal-fired grills. As a result, most foods will take a little longer to cook on a gas grill, and some of the more delicate foods, such as fish and vegetables, will be easier to cook to perfection.

While there are some who might say that attaching the label "gourmet" to gas-grilled food is stretching both the definition of the word "gourmet" and the capability of gas grills, after more than a year of experimenting with a great many grills and an even greater variety of foods, I'm convinced that food prepared on a gas grill can, indeed, be gourmet. I hope you'll agree that the 200 recipes in this book go a long way in proving me right.

THE GAS GRILL

❖◆❖

The first gas grills were introduced to consumers in 1961 by Charmglow. The earliest models were meant to be permanently installed, fueled not by an LP-gas cylinder, but by a direct link to a residential gas line. The first gas grills were large and quite costly, and they were considered luxury items.

Local gas-utility companies, quick to spot an up-and-coming trend (not to mention increased use of their product), took an interest in promoting gas grills to their residential customers. When the gas crunch hit in the early 1970s, the utility companies reversed themselves, issuing a moratorium on all nonessential natural gas–burning appliances such as pool heaters and, of course, gas grills.

Manufacturers of gas grills were quick to switch to LP-gas cylinders as a source of fuel, resulting in the sophisticated—and smaller, more mobile—units we see in the marketplace today. Interestingly, there now is a trend toward outfitting new residential homes with permanent natural gas hookups for gas grills, proving, once again, that what goes around comes around.

Each year consumers are offered increasingly sophisticated gas grills. Accessories range from multiple main and side burners, rotisseries, and warming racks, to built-in fish grids, smoking drawers, and containers for water to make steaming or moist-cooking possible. A choice of radiant materials, including lava rocks, ceramic briquets, and metal plates, is now available. Although the majority of grills sold today are in the $150 to $400 range, there has been a significant increase in the premium gas grill market, with some grills selling for $2000 and even up to $5000!

What should you look for in a gas grill? As with any piece of equipment, sound fundamentals are more important than the number of flashy extras. For starters, do not skimp on the size of the cooking surface. As you gain more experience at gas grilling, you are likely to want to cook several dishes simultaneously, including not just entrées but also appetizers, side dishes, and desserts. I recommend a minimum cooking area of 350 square inches, and, preferably, 400 square inches or more.

Look for a grill made of a relatively heavy-gauge metal that either resists rust or has a rust-resistant coating. Some grills have a rust-resistant main unit but other parts (legs, wheels, supports for swing-up racks, burners, and so on) that may rust. For optimum protection, spend the extra money for a first-rate, snug-fitting weatherproof covering from your grill's manufacturer. When your neighbors replace their grill after two or three years while yours still looks new, you will appreciate the investment you made.

Although every experienced griller learns that his or her grill has "hot spots," where the heat is highest, the less you need to think about them the better. Therefore, you should ask your dealer about how quickly and evenly the grill spreads heat. This is a function of the quality of metal in the main grill box, the grill's shape, the radiant material (lava rocks, ceramic briquets, or metal plates) that spreads the heat around, and the placement of the burners relative to the radiant material.

One of the first things you will learn about any grill is the number of BTUs (British thermal units) it delivers. Do not fall prey to the illusion that more BTUs are always better. Like a high-horsepower car, a grill with a particularly high number of BTUs may have you burning fuel at a hefty clip, a wasteful and expensive proposition. For a typical-size gas grill, you will want somewhere between 20,000 and 50,000 BTUs, and you might opt for the higher end of the scale if you think you will be grilling often in cold or windy weather. But what is more important than the gross number of BTUs is the efficiency with which the grill heats and cooks. Ask your dealer to make a case to you for the efficiency of the unit you are considering, and, if a particularly efficient unit means an extra fifty dollars or so up front, know that you will eventually save more than that in fuel costs.

Two or three main burners are desirable, especially for indirect cooking (see below), and those are the standard numbers available on most grills sold today. Buy a one-burner grill only if you need a particularly small and portable one, but do not get one if you will be keeping the grill in one place.

Side burners are good for boiling marinades and keeping them hot, for keeping finished food warm, and for cooking off-the-grill side dishes. They will, however, add a not insignificant amount to the cost of the grill. If your grill is situated at a fair distance from your kitchen, or if your family demands that you not heat up the kitchen on the nights you grill, a side burner or two may be a good idea. Side burners should always come with sturdy metallic covers that protect them when they are not in use.

Swing-up or fixed side shelves and work tables are nice, but even on the largest units they rarely give you all the working space you will need. I highly recommend having a separate, freestanding auxiliary table—preferably one with a heatproof surface material—near your grill for laying out utensils, cutting boards, and bowls of rubs or marinades. In addition, you can

use the table as a place to serve hot-off-the-grill appetizers. If you opt for side surfaces, make sure any wood they include is waterproofed well, either by the manufacturer or by you.

Many grills these days come with one or more of: condiment racks, towel bars, and utensil hooks. These accessories add little to the cost of the grill, so there is no reason to avoid them. I would not, however, make any of them the deciding feature, especially if you keep a separate table nearby. Chances are you'll have more utensils than you can hook up to your grill, and many of them won't hang from hooks anyway!

Your best and simplest rule of thumb when shopping for a gas grill is to be what car dealers call a "tire-kicker." Lift and lower the lid a few times to see if the hinges are wobble-free and smooth, and make sure that when the lid is completely open it stays in place. If you are on the short side, try the following test: Grab the lid handle with your hand, swing the lid completely up, and make sure that once the lid is up the metal front edge of the lid does not bump up against your wrist or forearm—an inconvenience you will definitely want to avoid when the grill is very hot.

Lift and lower any swing-up shelves, too, and put some pressure with your hand on all shelves and work surfaces to make sure they are sturdy, steady, and flat. Roll the unit back and forth a little to see if the wheels work well. Stand by the grill and check to see if the various knobs, handles, racks, and shelves are at a convenient height for you when you stand by the unit. Stand back from the grill a few feet to see if all the surfaces that are supposed to be parallel to the ground really are.

If you get less-than-satisfying results on any of these tests and your dealer tells you it is because the stock clerk did not assemble the grill properly, take *that* as a sign of potential trouble. It may mean that you, too, will have difficulty assembling the grill, and it almost certainly means that if you choose to pay the dealer to assemble the unit for you it will not be done right.

Finally, if you are replacing an old gas grill with a new one, and you use propane and not natural gas, get yourself a new main and spare tank, even if they do not come with the grill and you have to pay extra. Propane tanks tend to develop rust, and the purchase of a new grill is a good occasion for replacing them. You may need new tanks, in any case, because gas fittings have changed in recent years and your old tanks may not hook up correctly.

DIRECT AND INDIRECT COOKING

••◆••

D irect cooking on a gas grill means cooking directly over the heat. Indirect cooking means placing the food to be cooked over a burner that has been turned off, leaving the other one or two burners on medium or high. (All but the smallest gas grills are equipped with more than one burner.) In indirect cooking, the lid of the grill is kept closed.

In most of the recipes given in this book, indirect cooking is recommended. The reason for this is twofold. First, indirect cooking virtually ensures that the food being cooked will not burn. Second, indirect cooking greatly reduces the incidence of fat dripping onto the burners and returning to the food via flare-ups and smoke.

Almost all experienced gas-grill cooks prefer the indirect cooking method. Indirect cooking may take a little longer, but once you give it a try you will appreciate the improvement in the quality of your grilled food and the greater control it gives you while you grill. For some foods you may want to place the food directly over the heat at the very beginning of the cooking time, to sear them, and for others you may want direct heat at the very end, for just a minute or two, to develop a nicely browned exterior. In most instances—and in most of the recipes in this book—even these brief periods of direct cooking are unnecessary, because the food will be sufficiently browned using the indirect method.

If your gas grill has only one burner, you can approximate indirect cooking by turning the burner on low. Or, if your one-burner grill is large enough, you can try covering half of the lava rocks or other radiant material with a double thickness of heavy-duty aluminum foil, and placing the food over this covered half. With this latter method, you may be able to keep the burner at medium.

Note that whether you are using the direct or the indirect

cooking method, your grill will need to be preheated, with all of the burners on high, for approximately ten to fifteen minutes. Preheating helps to burn off any food residue from previous meals that has adhered to the cooking grate or the radiant material, and it brings the grill up to a temperature that will cook food properly, without sticking.

COOKING TIMES

.•◆•.

Many, many variables affect the cooking time of gas-grilled food. The outside air temperature and the level of wind will change the temperature in the grill, in the directions you would predict but, in my experience at least, more dramatically than you might expect. Just as much variation comes from your grill itself: the types of burners and radiant material in your particular model; the shape and size of the grill; the distance from the burners or radiant materials to the cooking grate; and, especially, the differences from one manufacturer or model to another in what the settings "high," "medium," and "low" mean.

Therefore, all of the cooking times given on the following pages are, by necessity, approximate ones. As many people do with their indoor ovens, you will get a feel for whether your grill cooks "hot"—more quickly—or "cool"—more slowly—relative to the recipe instructions that follow, and you can make adjustments accordingly. Feel free to note your adjustments in the margins; just don't do so in a copy you have borrowed from a friend or the local library!

To avoid adding even more variability in cooking times, try to keep to a minimum the number of times you open the grill's lid when you are cooking. Every time you do so you lose heat and add to the cooking time. A good instant-read thermometer for testing the doneness of meats will help.

Keep in mind that it is always better to err on the side of undercooking rather than overcooking. Any food can easily be returned to the grill for more cooking, but there is little you can do if you have overcooked your food.

GENERAL GRILLING GUIDELINES
.•◆•.

Always start with the best possible ingredients, whether it's a tomato, a salmon fillet, or a beef tenderloin. Grilling is a very simple form of cooking, and, as such, there is little to mask or improve the flavor of less than the best and freshest of ingredients.

• Allow food to come to room temperature before grilling. Generally speaking, this means removing it from the refrigerator approximately twenty to thirty minutes prior to cooking.

• Always preheat your grill for approximately ten to fifteen minutes prior to grilling. Preheat with the burners on high, and with the lid down.

• As a rule, do not partially cook vegetables before grilling. Parboiling, steaming, or microwaving produce prior to grilling will result in a mushy, inferior texture.

• When in doubt, use a meat thermometer. It offers the easiest and most reliable way of determining the doneness of any meat or poultry.

SAFETY
.•◆•.

Gas grills are remarkably safe to use, but only if they are used properly. Take the time to read through the owner's manual that came with your gas grill, making special note of any safety precautions specific to your equipment. For whatever grill you own, the following guidelines are worth keeping in mind:

• Gas grills are intended for outdoor use only. Do not use your grill in a building, garage, screened or unscreened porch, or semienclosed area, on a balcony, or under a ceiling, overhang, or other cover. Do not install gas grills on a recreational vehicle or boat. Always keep the area around and under the grill clear of any combustible materials.

• Do not locate the grill on an uneven or unstable surface. Do not place the grill on a sidewalk or path.

• Do not store or use flammable vapors and liquids, such as gasoline, near your gas grill.

• LP-gas cylinders should be stored outdoors, in an area where the temperature never exceeds 125° F. If exposed to high temperatures, the relief valve may open, allowing flammable gas to escape.

• Do not store an auxiliary LP-gas cylinder in the vicinity of the gas grill, and do not store it in a building, garage, or other enclosed or semienclosed area.

• Always transport, store, and use LP cylinders in an upright position.

• Do not disconnect gas fittings or valves while the grill is in use.

• Make sure the lid of the grill is open before lighting the burners.

• Do not leave the grill unattended while it is in use.

• Do not move the grill while it is lit.

• Do not block air to the grill or to the ventilation openings. Do not use lump charcoal in your grill; it will break down and plug the ventilation holes.

• To avoid bacterial contamination, use different cutting or carving boards, and different platters, for raw foods and cooked or finished ones. Any marinade that will be reused in a finishing or table sauce must first be boiled fully.

• Do not wear loose-fitting clothes (sleeves, especially) when you grill.

• Do not let children operate or play near the grill. (It's a good idea to keep pets away from a hot grill, too.)

• If you smell gas, shut off the gas to the grill, extinguish any open flame, and open the lid to the grill. If the odor continues, immediately call your gas supplier or your local fire department.

• Never check for gas leaks with a lighted match or open flame. A good way to test for leaks is to keep a spray bottle full of soapy water on hand; spray the joints or fittings, and if you can see bubbles forming you have a leak. Repair or replace the leaking parts promptly. Test for leaks the first couple of times you use a new grill, and on a regular basis as your grill gets up in years.

• If a burner does not light, turn off the gas, wait five minutes, and try again. The problem may be a blockage in your grill's venturi tube. Check your owner's manual for instructions on cleaning it out.

• Always make sure the LP-cylinder valve is closed when the grill is not in use.

• Have dented or rusty gas cylinders inspected by your propane dealer. If the rust or dents are severe, replace the tank.

• If you are discarding and not refilling an old tank, do so according to the safety and waste-handling regulations in your community. Remember that while an "empty" tank may have no more liquid in it, it does have flammable vapors.

ACCESSORIES

·◆·

Great grilling starts with a solid, reliable grill. Beyond that, the list of accessories most grillers find truly useful is mercifully short:

• **Spatula.** Get one with a long handle and with a thin and flexible, but not too floppy, blade, which will be ideal for sliding under delicate foods like vegetables and fish. Offset spatulas, with the blade lower than the handle, work particularly well in grilling.

• **Basting brushes.** For fast and easy basting, paintbrushes from the hardware store work great, especially ones about 2½ inches wide. Because it is not easy to clean brushes on the fly, I recommend you keep at least two on hand, for meals with different sauces for different dishes. Otherwise, your sauces may get mixed together.

• **Forks.** You will need a large chef's or carving fork or two if you will be grilling larger roasts or birds. Find the best quality ones you can—long-handled, extra-sturdy, and with sharp tines. Do keep the tines sharp. With dull ones you will have to force the fork farther into the meat to get a grip, and that will lead to the draining of flavorful juices.

• **Spring-loaded tongs.** Again, get the best-quality and heaviest-duty ones you can find. Although long tongs are useful, the laws of physics say that the longer the tongs the more effort you will have to expend when you use them to lift something heavy, like a roast. I prefer using medium-length (12 inches or so) tongs, along with a great pair of gloves or mitts.

- **Gloves.** Of all the grilling and barbecue accessories available these days, heat-resistant gloves are the ones that most commonly disappoint the experienced griller. Grilling suppliers typically offer what are standard kitchen mitts with an extra couple of inches of length, barely covering the wrist, and with scarcely any extra heat protection. If you live in or near a large city, do what Cheryl and Bill Jamison, authors of the definitive books on smoke-cooked barbecue, *Smoke & Spice* and *Sublime Smoke*, recommend: stop by a firefighters' supply store and get yourself a pair of truly protective, elbow-length neoprene gloves. If you cannot find these, do get the longest and most heat-resistant gloves you can find.

- **Instant-read meat thermometer.** This is an indispensable tool if you will be cooking larger items like roasts or whole birds. Get one that is sturdy and has a sharp insert.

- **Skewers, both bamboo and metal.** Have plenty on hand, especially if you entertain, and do not forget to soak bamboo ones before you use them. Some kebob pros favor two-pronged skewers, which keep the skewered food from spinning around. These come in metal but not disposable bamboo, so if you opt for these you will have to wash them after meals.

- **Grids, racks, baskets.** Grill grates are designed for the big, sturdy old standards, like burgers and steaks. For smaller or more delicate foods, you will want to own a separate grid or rack with smaller openings. The rack will simply sit atop your built-in cooking grate. Wire baskets, with hinges and a handle, will serve you well if you cook whole fish or fish fillets; you can turn the fish and remove it from the heat without fear of it sticking to the grate or breaking apart and falling into the grill. Fish baskets are indispensable if you will be cooking any skin-on fish.

- *Two* **large cutting boards.** Save yourself cleanup trips to the kitchen by keeping one board for cutting raw foods and one for finished dishes.

- **Marinating bowls.** Make sure these are made of glass or another nonreactive material. Have at least one on hand that is quite wide and deep.

- **Cleaning brush.** Get one with stiff bristles, such as brass. Do follow your grill manufacturer's recommendations, particularly if you own a model with a cooking grate made of porcelain-coated steel, which can chip. Grill dealers sell brushes that are designed for cleaning porcelain.

• **Lighting.** If you have not yet outfitted your cooking area with an overhead light for cooking at night, a clip lamp or a flashlight will come in handy.

• **Lots of heavy-duty aluminum foil.** You will find this useful, especially if you do not own separate racks or baskets, for holding small and delicate foods in place on the grill. If your grill has a warming rack for foods that are done cooking, an extra layer or two of foil under or around the food will keep it moist and give you more insurance against overcooking. Foil is also helpful for containing wood chips or other aromatics. Some grilling aficionados swear that the best cooking-grate cleaner is crinkled-up foil; it certainly works well, but the catch is that the easiest time for cleaning a grate is when it is still hot, and you will need to be careful.

• **Spare gas tank.** If there is one immutable law of gas grilling, it is that the most likely time for you to run out of propane is on a Sunday evening, when there's a small horde of hungry guests waiting to eat and no propane dealer is open for business.

WOOD CHIPS

O ne of the easiest ways to add flavor to gas-grilled food is to add wood chips to the inside of the grill when you cook. As the chips smolder in the heat, they will infuse your food with a smoky flavor reminiscent of old-fashioned barbecue. But note that while in traditional smoke-cooked barbecue wood is both a flavor enhancer and a fuel, in gas grilling it is solely a flavoring agent. In a gas grill, the gas burners are the primary heat source.

The recipes in this book do not call for using wood chips or other smoke-producing aromatics. The marinades, herb and spice combinations, and sauces in the recipes will yield full-flavored dishes without the need for extra help. Although wood chips now are widely available at gourmet stores and grill dealerships, and by mail-order, I have also avoided calling for them because the chances are fair that on a given night you will not have on hand the particular type of wood that pairs with the food you are cooking. Many grocery stores and supermarkets do not carry chips, so it is possible that you would be in for an extra shopping expedition if the recipes demanded them.

Nonetheless, using wood chips is a fun way to expand your grilling skills. Use wood chips only when you are cooking indirectly, with the lid closed. Wood chips can ignite, of course, so always check your owner's manual first for directions on how to use them safely with your grill. You must soak the chips beforehand, for thirty minutes or so. You must contain them, too, either in a special aluminum or cast-iron box—usually called a "smoker box"—sold as an accessory by grill dealers, in a similar box or drawer that is built into your grill, or by wrapping them in a double thickness of heavy-duty aluminum foil (perforate the foil numerous times with a fork to create holes through which the smoke can escape).

Some grills will accommodate a box that holds larger chunks of wood; again, check your manual to see if using wood chunks is recommended. Chips provide a sufficient amount of smoke for smaller foods or foods that cook in shorter times. Larger chunks, which last longer, come in handy for more substantial pieces of food, such as roasts or whole birds, with longer cooking times.

If you do decide to experiment with wood-smoke flavoring, you'll add a whole new dimension to your grilling repertoire, and, with practice, you'll even be able to approximate the skills of a venerable Southern pitmaster. To get you started, here are the more common types of wood available, along with the foods with which they go best:

ALDER: Traditionally pairs with seafood, especially salmon. Also excellent with pork and chicken.

APPLE: A sweet flavor very good with ham and sausage, and good with other pork dishes, along with poultry and game birds.

CHERRY: Great with duck and very good with chicken and turkey. Pairs handsomely with lamb and venison, too.

HICKORY: The traditional wood for Southern-style pork barbecue, but perfectly appropriate for beef and poultry as well.

MAPLE: Traditional, of course, with cured or cold-smoked ham, and very fine, too, with grilled ham. A good complement for turkey and some vegetables, such as squash.

MESQUITE: Not a traditional barbecue wood, but popular in recent years, to say the least. Use sparingly and not over a long cooking time, to avoid a bitter flavor. Goes well with pork or lamb chops, beef steaks, and swordfish, and, used modestly, with vegetables.

OAK: Great with steaks and other beef dishes, and does nice things for duck and all manner of pork.

PECAN: Subtle, mild, and versatile, good with poultry, pork, and beef.

SASSAFRAS: Used sparingly, provides a nice, sweet touch for poultry, pork, and seafood.

Always avoid softwoods, such as pines and other evergreens, which are too bitter for smoke flavoring, and by all means avoid chemical-laden chips derived from pressure-treated lumber or any wood that has ever been finished or painted.

Some grilling aficionados get tasty results with grapevines, nutshells, cinnamon sticks, tea bags, citrus peels, and herbs, both leaves and twigs. As with wood chips, you must soak thoroughly any of these items that are flammable and contain them in a smoker box or foil packet. Experimenting with materials like these makes for an interesting way to recycle what otherwise might be kitchen waste. Start with small quantities used over a short portion of the grilling time, so that you do not overwhelm the flavor of your food.

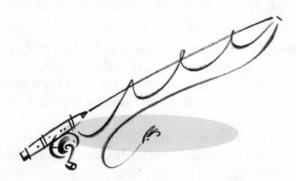

THE GAS GRILL
GOURMET

CHAPTER ONE

♦

APPETIZERS

♦

CHAPTER ONE
APPETIZERS

⋄◆⋄

Grilling involves a little bit of theater. There's something attractive and entertaining about cooking over an open fire that makes people want to be part of the action. Maybe it's because most grilling takes place outdoors, or because cooking over live heat has a primal appeal, or simply because grilling is a relaxed, informal activity that invites camaraderie. Whatever the reason, why not reward your family and friends for their good company with a little something while they're waiting for the main course? As your guests stand around the grill and watch you prepare these tasty tidbits, they will feel as if they're really part of the event. After all, inviting family and friends to your home for a meal isn't called entertaining for nothing.

The following recipes take little time to prepare and even less time to grill. Some, like Grilled Cheese on a Skewer, will appeal to everyone, young and old alike. Others, like Grilled Oysters with Fresh Ginger Vinaigrette, will attract those with more sophisticated palates.

Appetizers made with grilled bread—whether Italian bruschetta or Mexican quesadilla—are universally popular. Indeed, more home cooks should try grilling breads on their gas grills. A simple grilled bread can be the perfect starter for an excellent meal.

Any type of bruschetta is best made with a coarse-textured Italian or French bread, which is becoming more widely available in all parts of the country. Don't worry if the bread isn't as fresh as possible: there's something about the grilling process that makes even slightly stale bread taste great. If a bruschetta recipe calls for olive oil, always use the best extra-virgin olive oil you can find. In recipes with only a few ingredients and such simple preparation methods, each ingredient must be a standout.

Whatever you choose to serve as an appetizer, remember that it should tease the appetite, not sate it. It's a good idea to serve only a small amount of any appetizer, just to guarantee that everyone will have room for the delicious meal still to come.

GRILLED GARLIC BREAD

It's hard to find anyone who dislikes garlic bread. These crusty slices are also good as an accompaniment to a main course.

1 large loaf coarse-textured Italian or French bread
About ¼ cup extra-virgin olive oil
4 to 6 garlic cloves, pressed

1. Preheat the grill for 10 to 15 minutes, with all the burners on high.

2. While the grill is preheating, cut the bread in half lengthwise. Combine the olive oil and garlic and lightly brush the mixture onto the cut sides of the bread.

3. Once the grill is hot, turn all the burners to low. Place the bread halves on the grill, cut sides up. Grill the bread, turning it once, until the halves are toasted on both sides. Watch closely, because the toasting will take only a few minutes.

4. Transfer the toast to a cutting board and cut the bread into individual slices. Serve warm.

Serves 4 to 6

BRUSCHETTA WITH SHAVED PARMESAN

Bruschetta starts with a rustic loaf of high-quality, coarse-textured Italian or French bread. The bread is brushed lightly with olive oil, then toasted on the grill. In this version, the bread gets a topping of Parmesan. This is about as simple as food gets, and about as good. All that's necessary are the finest possible ingredients: crusty Italian or French bread, Parmigiano-Reggiano, and a first-rate, extra-virgin olive oil. Serve with a dry red wine for a real taste treat. One small loaf will yield about 12 slices, a baguette about 16 slices.

Just about any vegetable that retains a little snap after grilling can be served as an appetizer with a dip. Try asparagus, carrots, or even potato wedges. See Chapter 7 for more instructions on grilling these and other vegetables.

1 loaf coarse-textured Italian or French bread
About ¼ cup extra-virgin olive oil
6-ounce chunk Parmesan cheese
1 large garlic clove, cut in half lengthwise

1. Preheat the grill for 10 to 15 minutes, with all the burners on high.

2. While the grill is preheating, cut the bread into ½-inch slices and lightly brush both sides of each slice with olive oil. Using a sharp knife, shave the Parmesan very thin—it may crumble somewhat—and reserve. Alternatively, you can grate the cheese on the coarse side of a box grater.

3. Once the grill is hot, turn all the burners to low. Place the bread slices on the grill and toast both sides, turning them once. Watch closely, because the toasting will take only a few minutes. Once the slices are toasted, rub each one quickly with the cut garlic.

4. Arrange the toasted bread on a platter, top with the reserved Parmesan, and serve warm.

Serves 6 to 8

TOMATO-BASIL BRUSCHETTA

At the height of summer, when vine-ripened tomatoes are at their peak, try this bruschetta, with its simple but absolutely delicious topping of ripe tomatoes and sweet basil. One small loaf will yield about 12 slices, a baguette about 16 slices.

1½ pounds red-ripe tomatoes
½ cup extra-virgin olive oil
1 cup minced fresh basil or parsley (or a combination of
* both)*
Salt and fresh-ground black pepper to taste
Balsamic vinegar to taste
1 loaf coarse-textured Italian or French bread
1 large garlic clove, cut in half lengthwise

1. Preheat the grill for 10 to 15 minutes, with all the burners on high.

2. While the grill is preheating, prepare the tomato-basil topping. Chop the tomatoes into small chunks and transfer them to a medium bowl. Add ¼ cup of the olive oil and the basil, parsley, or both. Add salt, pepper, and a dash of balsamic vinegar to taste. Let the mixture stand at room temperature until serving time.

3. Cut the bread into ½-inch slices, and brush both sides of each slice with the remaining olive oil.

4. Once the grill is hot, turn all the burners to low. Place the bread slices on the grill and toast both sides, turning them once. Watch closely, because the toasting will take only a few minutes. Once the slices are done, rub each one quickly with the cut garlic.

5. Place the toasted bread on a platter. Using a slotted spoon, top each slice with some of the tomato-basil mixture. Serve immediately—and be prepared to make more!

Serves 6 to 12

•◆•

GORGONZOLA TOASTS

•◆•

This is a variation on a wonderful hors d'oeuvre originated by the great Italian cookbook author Marcella Hazan. It's a real crowd pleaser, so make plenty.

½ cup crumbled Gorgonzola cheese
½ cup grated mozzarella cheese
2 tablespoons pine nuts, toasted in a dry skillet for about
  3 minutes until golden
1 garlic clove, pressed
Fresh-ground black pepper to taste
1 loaf coarse-textured Italian or French bread
About ¼ cup extra-virgin olive oil

1. Preheat the grill for 10 to 15 minutes, with all the burners on high.

2. While the grill is preheating, combine the cheeses, pine nuts, garlic, and pepper in a bowl. Toss the mixture lightly with a fork and let stand at room temperature until needed.

3. Cut the bread into ½-inch slices, and lightly brush each slice on both sides with olive oil.

4. Once the grill is hot, turn all the burners to low. Place the bread slices on the grill and toast on one side only. Watch closely, because the toasting will take only a minute. Turn the bread pieces and top each one with the cheese mixture, pressing down on it slightly with a fork. Close the grill's lid and bake the toasts for a few minutes, until the cheese mixture has melted.

5. Serve the toasts hot off the grill.

Serves 6 to 8

••◆••
GRILLED CHEESE ON A SKEWER
••◆••

These bite-size, skewered grilled cheese sandwiches are simple but satisfying. If you feel like taking the recipe a step further, you can insert small slices of smoked ham (or prosciutto) between the slices of bread and cheese for a variation on that French specialty *croque monsieur*.

1 large loaf coarse-textured French or Italian bread
About ½ pound Gruyère, Emmenthaler, or Monterey jack
  cheese
6 bamboo skewers, soaked in water
About 2 tablespoons extra-virgin olive oil

1. Preheat the grill for 10 to 15 minutes, with all the burners on high.

2. While the grill is preheating, prepare the bread and cheese. Remove the crust from the loaf of bread, cut the bread into ¾-inch slices, and then cut each slice into pieces about 2 inches square. Cut the cheese into slices that are ¼ inch thick and about 2 inches square.

3. Thread the bread and cheese squares onto the skewers:

begin with bread, add cheese and bread in turn, and end with bread. Brush the skewered bread and cheese with olive oil.

4. Once the grill is hot, turn one burner off and turn the other(s) to medium. Position the skewered bread and cheese over the burner that is off. Close the grill's lid and cook the skewers for approximately 8 to 10 minutes, turning them several times, until the bread is lightly toasted on all sides and the cheese has melted.

5. Transfer the food to your work surface and pull out each skewer. Place the "loaves" of grilled bread and cheese on a platter. Tear off individual slices, and pass the Dijon mustard, please!

Serves 6 to 8

◆

CHEESE QUESADILLAS

◆

This is a great, quick appetizer. If the flavors are too plain for you, then mix in with the cheese chopped fresh cilantro, chili powder, chopped green onions, or diced peppers, from the mildest bell to the hottest habanero. Use your imagination.

> *Four 10-inch flour tortillas*
> *About 2 tablespoons vegetable oil*
> *2 cups grated Monterey jack or mild cheddar cheese (or a*
>   *combination of both)*
> *Hot sauce, salsa, or chopped fresh cilantro (optional)*

1. Preheat the grill for 10 to 15 minutes, with all the burners on high.

2. While the grill is preheating, assemble the quesadillas. Lightly brush 2 of the tortillas with some of the vegetable oil on one side. Place the tortillas next to each other, oiled side down, on your work surface. Top each one with 1 cup of cheese, and then cover each with another tortilla. Press down lightly to compress the cheese. Lightly brush the top of each quesadilla with the remaining oil.

3. Once the grill is hot, turn all the burners to low. Using a spatula, carefully place each quesadilla on the grill. Watch closely: as soon as the cheese begins to melt, press down lightly on each quesadilla with the spatula and turn it over to brown the other side. The quesadillas will be done when they are lightly browned on both sides and the cheese is completely melted.

4. Transfer the cooked quesadillas to a cutting board and, using a large, sharp knife, slice each one into 4 to 6 pie-shaped wedges. If you wish, top the wedges with hot sauce, salsa, or a sprinkling of chopped fresh cilantro. Serve warm.

Serves 4 to 6

CHEESE-STUFFED GRAPE LEAVES

Around the world, wherever grapes are grown, cooks wrap a variety of foods in grape leaves before grilling: everything from meat and rice to fish or cheese. Not only do the leaves keep what's inside them from falling apart, they impart their own unique, piquant, somewhat lemony flavor. If you're fortunate enough to live within picking distance of a grape vine, use fresh leaves. Just be sure to destem them and blanch them in boiling water for 4 to 5 minutes. When finding fresh leaves is out of the question, use bottled grape leaves, which are readily available at specialty food shops and are easy to work with. This recipe makes an unusual and delicious appetizer, certain to elicit lots of comments.

8-ounce jar grape leaves in brine
About 1 pound cheese, such as Monterey jack, fontina,
    brie, or Teleme
About 3 tablespoons extra-virgin olive oil
Balsamic vinegar to taste
1 baguette, cut in thin slices (optional)

1. Rinse the grape leaves, drain them well, and blot them dry. Discard any very small or torn leaves. Cut the cheese into rectangles about 1½ inches by 2 inches and ⅜ inch thick.

2. Preheat the grill for 10 to 15 minutes, with all the burners on high.

3. While the grill is preheating, stuff the grape leaves. To begin, place a grape leaf on your work surface, vein side up. Place a piece of cheese in the center of the leaf. Wrap the leaf around the cheese as if you were wrapping a package, folding in the stem side first. Then place the stuffed leaf on another leaf and make a secure bundle. Repeat with the remaining cheese and leaves. Finally, brush each bundle with olive oil.

4. Once the grill is hot, turn one burner off and turn the other(s) to medium. Put the grape leaves in a hinged grill basket and place the basket over the burner that is off. Close the grill's lid and cook, turning the grill basket once or twice, until the cheese has melted, approximately 15 minutes (taste one stuffed leaf to check).

5. Transfer the stuffed leaves to a platter. Douse them with balsamic vinegar and serve by themselves or on top of thin slices of crusty bread.

Serves 8 to 12

◆

RACLETTE IN A BOWL

◆

Traditional raclette is a Swiss cheese that has been melted in a special broiler unit and is served with boiled new potatoes, pickled onions, and gherkins. This variation requires nothing more than your gas grill and 4 to 6 small, shallow, heat-proof bowls.

> *2 pounds new potatoes, well scrubbed (or substitute about 2 dozen small pieces of toasted, crunchy French or Italian bread)*
> *1¼ pounds raclette, Swiss, Emmenthaler, Gruyère, or fontina cheese, grated*
> *Pickled onions and cornichons or gherkins*

1. Boil the potatoes in salted water to cover until they are tender, about 15 minutes. Drain the potatoes and cut them in half. (If you're substituting bread for the potatoes, proceed to step 2.)

2. Preheat the grill for 10 to 15 minutes, with all the burners on high.

3. While the grill is preheating, divide the grated cheese among the small bowls. Cover each with aluminum foil.

4. Once the grill is hot, turn one burner off and turn the other(s) to medium. Place the covered, cheese-filled bowls over the burner that is off. Close the grill's lid and cook the cheese for approximately 10 minutes. Once the cheese has melted, remove the foil and continue to cook just until the cheese starts to bubble at the edges.

5. Serve the cheese in the bowls hot off the grill, using the potatoes or the bread to dip, accompanied with the pickles.

Serves 4 to 6

⋅⋅◆⋅⋅
MARINATED MUSHROOMS AND CHERRY TOMATOES
⋅⋅◆⋅⋅

G rilled marinated mushrooms and cherry tomatoes are delicious hot or cold, by themselves or as a topping for Grilled Garlic Bread (page 4). Any way you serve them, they make a wonderful snack.

MARINADE
½ cup dry red wine
¼ cup extra-virgin olive oil
Juice of ½ lemon
1 large garlic clove, pressed
2 teaspoons dried thyme leaves, crumbled
1 teaspoon salt
½ teaspoon fresh-cracked peppercorns

*1 pound whole mushrooms, well scrubbed and stems
   trimmed*
1 pound cherry tomatoes
12 bamboo skewers, soaked in water

Slices of toasted bread (optional)

1. Combine the marinade ingredients in a large, nonreactive bowl and mix well. Toss the mushrooms and the cherry tomatoes in the marinade. Cover the bowl and refrigerate for 1 to 2 hours.

2. Preheat the grill for 10 to 15 minutes, with all the burners on high.

3. While the grill is preheating, drain off the marinade and discard it. Thread the mushrooms onto 6 skewers and the cherry tomatoes onto another 6.

4. Once the grill is hot, turn one burner off and turn the other(s) to medium. Position the skewers of mushrooms and tomatoes over the burner that is off. Close the grill's lid and cook for approximately 8 to 10 minutes, turning the skewers occasionally. Depending on their size, the mushrooms will be tender in about 8 to 12 minutes. The tomatoes will be done when they are heated all the way through and are soft to the touch.

5. Serve the mushrooms and tomatoes hot off the grill, or toss them together in a bowl and serve at room temperature, on slices of crunchy, toasted bread if desired.

Serves 6 to 8

MIXED GRILLED VEGETABLES WITH FETA CHEESE DIP

This variation on the ubiquitous raw-vegetables-and-dip platter can be served warm or cold. Grilling intensifies the flavors of the vegetables, and the feta cheese dip is fresh-tasting and relatively low in calories and fat.

DIP
1 cup sour cream
¾ cup crumbled feta cheese
2 cloves garlic, pressed
1 tablespoon red or white wine vinegar
2 tablespoons minced fresh parsley
Fresh-ground black pepper to taste

1 red bell pepper, seeded and deveined, cut in 1-inch squares

1 green bell pepper, seeded and deveined, cut in 1-inch squares
2 onions, cut in 1-inch cubes
18 cherry tomatoes or 9 yellow pear tomatoes, halved
18 button mushrooms, well scrubbed and stems trimmed
1 small to medium unpeeled zucchini or other summer squash, cut in 1-inch cubes
12 bamboo skewers, soaked in water
About ½ cup extra-virgin olive oil
Salt and fresh-ground black pepper to taste
2 tablespoons fresh thyme or 2 teaspoons dried thyme leaves

1. In a bowl, combine all the dip ingredients and mix well. Cover the bowl and refrigerate until needed.

2. Preheat the grill for 10 to 15 minutes, with all the burners on high.

3. While the grill is preheating, thread the vegetables onto the bamboo skewers in an alternating pattern. Make sure to pierce the mushrooms through the cap, so they don't fall apart, and skewer the zucchini through the skin, so all the cut sides face outward. Coat the vegetables with a liberal amount of olive oil, salt, and pepper, and sprinkle them with the thyme.

4. Once the grill is hot, turn one burner off and turn the other(s) to medium. Position the brochettes over the burner that is off, close the grill's lid, and cook for about 8 to 12 minutes, turning the vegetables occasionally. The vegetables will be done when the tip of a sharp knife easily pierces them but they still have a little crunch.

5. Serve the vegetables hot off the grill, accompanied with the feta cheese dip.

Serves 6 to 12

⁎⬧⁎
GRILLED SCALLOP CEVICHE
⁎⬧⁎

Ceviche—raw fish or shellfish "cooked" in a highly acidic marinade, usually composed of citrus juices—is a popular appetizer in Mexico. Besides "cooking" them, the marinade imbues the fish and shellfish with very distinct and spicy (although not necessarily "hot" spicy) flavors. It takes at least 4 hours to fully "cook" the fish and shellfish in the citrus juice marinade; in this recipe, the scallops marinate for a maximum of 2 hours and finish cooking on the grill. It's a delightful combination of cooking techniques and flavors. You can also serve these scallops as an alternative filling for Fish Tacos (page 48).

MARINADE
¼ cup fresh lime juice
¼ cup fresh lemon juice
¼ cup fresh orange juice
1 small onion, diced
3 tablespoons light vegetable oil, such as canola
¼ cup minced fresh cilantro
¼ teaspoon dried oregano
½ teaspoon hot pepper sauce
¼ teaspoon salt

2 pounds sea scallops
12 bamboo skewers, soaked in water

Lemon wedges and chopped fresh cilantro, for garnish
   (optional)

1. Combine all the marinade ingredients in a medium-size glass or ceramic bowl and mix well. Wash the scallops in cold water and blot dry. Add the scallops to the marinade, cover the bowl, and refrigerate for approximately 2 hours.

2. Preheat the grill for 10 to 15 minutes, with all the burners on high.

3. While the grill is preheating, drain off the marinade and discard it. Thread the scallops, with their sides touching, onto the skewers.

4. Once the grill is hot, turn all the burners to medium-high. Grill the skewered scallops for 2 to 3 minutes, turning once. Remove the scallops from the grill just as soon as the meat turns opaque white.

5. Serve immediately, with lemon wedges and a sprinkling of cilantro, if desired.

Serves 6 to 8 generously

SKEWERED SHRIMP WITH LEMON AND BASIL

On their own, these shrimp make an outstanding (and hearty) appetizer. On top of pasta tossed with a little garlic, olive oil, and chopped fresh parsley, they make a tangy, tasty main dish. Add some warm, crusty bread and a glass of white wine and you've got yourself a meal-size treat.

MARINADE
⅓ cup extra-virgin olive oil
½ cup dry white wine
2 tablespoons fresh lemon juice
½ cup minced fresh basil
3 large garlic cloves, pressed
Fresh-ground black pepper to taste

2 pounds large or jumbo shrimp, peeled, deveined, and
*   rinsed in cold water*
2 dozen bamboo skewers, soaked in water

1. Combine all the marinade ingredients in a large, nonreactive bowl and mix well. Add the prepared shrimp, cover the bowl, and refrigerate for about 1 hour.

2. Preheat the grill for 10 to 15 minutes, with all the burners on high.

3. While the grill is preheating, drain off the marinade and discard it. Skewer the shrimp by threading them on two parallel

To help ensure uniform cooking, make pieces of food destined for skewers as uniform in size as possible.

skewers. This will keep the shrimp from spinning around when you turn them on the grill.

4. Once the grill is hot, turn one burner off and turn the other(s) to medium. Position the shrimp over the burner that is off, close the grill's lid, and cook for about 6 to 8 minutes, turning once. Do not overcook: the shrimp will be done just as soon as they turn opaque on both sides and are firm to the touch.

5. Serve immediately.

Serves 8 to 10

⋅⋅◆⋅⋅
"BARBECUED" OYSTERS
⋅⋅◆⋅⋅

Grilled oysters are great party food, especially when you need some entertainment out by the grill, because that's exactly where these appetizers should be enjoyed. Be forewarned: The world is divided between those who will try one oyster just to be a good sport and those who can down a couple of dozen without thinking twice. So when it comes to figuring out how many oysters to buy, *caveat emptor.*

About 2 dozen fresh oysters, or more
Your favorite bottled barbecue sauce, heated

1. Scrub the oysters under cold running water and store them, flat shells up, in a cool place until you are ready to grill.

2. Preheat the grill for 10 to 15 minutes, with all the burners on high.

3. Once the grill is hot, turn all the burners to medium. Place the oysters, flat shells up, directly over the burners. Close the grill's lid and cook for approximately 4 to 5 minutes, then take a peek. The oysters will be done as soon as their shells pop open slightly; some may take a little longer to open than others.

4. Transfer the oysters to your work surface. Using an oyster knife, remove the top shell of each oyster and discard. Pour a dab or two of barbecue sauce on top of each oyster. Put the oysters back on the grill just until the sauce starts to bubble at the edges.

5. Serve immediately, on the half shell.

Serves 4 to 6

⋅◆⋅

GRILLED OYSTERS WITH FRESH GINGER VINAIGRETTE

⋅◆⋅

Grilled fresh oysters are about as festive as an appetizer can get. When you grill them directly over the fire, the oysters even pop open on their own, so you don't have to pry those tight shells apart. Although lemon juice, grated horseradish, and bottled hot sauce are traditional—and delicious—accompaniments to oysters, this recipe offers a fresh alternative.

3 dozen fresh oysters

VINAIGRETTE
½ cup rice wine vinegar
Juice of 1 lemon
4 tablespoons grated fresh ginger
Tabasco sauce to taste

1. Scrub the oysters under cold running water and store them, flat shells up, in a cool place until you are ready to grill.

2. In a small, nonreactive bowl, combine the vinaigrette ingredients and mix well. Cover the bowl and refrigerate until needed.

3. Preheat the grill for 10 to 15 minutes, with all the burners on high.

4. Once the grill is hot, turn all the burners to medium. Place the oysters, flat shells up, directly over the burners. Close the grill's lid and cook for approximately 4 to 5 minutes, then take a peek. The oysters will be done as soon as their shells pop open slightly; some may take a little longer to open than others.

5. Transfer the oysters to your work surface. Using an oyster knife, remove each oyster's top shell and discard. Serve the oysters immediately, with the bowl of fresh ginger vinaigrette close by.

Serves 6 to 9

SKEWERED CHICKEN LIVERS WITH FRESH LIME AND CILANTRO

This is an unusual combination, but one that works exceedingly well, especially as an appetizer. For a dish so simple, the flavors are surprisingly complex and pleasing: the piquant lime juice complements the richness of the chicken livers beautifully, and the cilantro adds a fresh, "green" flavor all its own. Because the livers cook up so quickly, you can grill them easily before the main course.

> *1 pound chicken livers*
> *4 bamboo skewers, soaked in water*
> *Vegetable oil*
> *Salt and fresh-ground black pepper to taste*
> *1 lime, quartered*
> *½ cup coarsely chopped fresh cilantro*

1. Preheat the grill for 10 to 15 minutes, with all the burners on high.

2. While the grill is preheating, rinse the chicken livers in cold water and dry them well. Thread or weave about 5 livers onto each skewer. Rub the meat with a little vegetable oil and then dust lightly with salt and pepper.

3. Once the grill is hot, turn all the burners to low. Place the skewered chicken livers on the grill, close the grill's lid, and cook for 7 to 9 minutes, turning them once.

4. Serve the livers hot off the grill, with the cilantro sprinkled over the top and the lime wedges on the side, ready for a good squeeze.

Serves 4 to 6

RUMAKI

This blast from the past was a standard hors d'oeuvre at cocktail parties circa 1960. A generation later, these chicken livers still taste good, especially hot off the grill. Far from snickering at such a passé canapé, your guests may embark on a vivid trip down memory lane.

18 bacon slices
½ pound chicken livers, washed, patted dry, and cut in
   1-inch cubes
About ¼ cup soy or teriyaki sauce
8-ounce can whole water chestnuts, rinsed and drained
6 to 12 bamboo skewers, soaked in water

1. Preheat the grill for 10 to 15 minutes, with all the burners on high.

2. While the grill is preheating, cut the bacon slices in half and fry them in a pan on the stove until they are about half cooked. Drain the bacon well on paper towels.

3. In a small bowl, combine the chicken livers with just enough soy or teriyaki sauce to cover, and let sit for 5 minutes. Pair one chicken liver cube and one water chestnut, wrapping the two with a piece of the partially cooked bacon. String as many as you can onto the bamboo skewers.

4. Once the grill is hot, turn one burner off and turn the other(s) to medium. Place the skewers over the burner that is off. Close the grill's lid and cook for 18 to 25 minutes, turning the skewers several times.

5. Serve the rumaki hot off the grill.

Serves 4 to 6

CHAPTER TWO

◆

FISH AND SHELLFISH

◆

CHAPTER TWO
FISH AND SHELLFISH

•٠◆٠•

ish has become so popular with Americans that it is now possible to buy an excellent, fresh assortment of fish in almost every part of the country. Preparing fish on a gas grill is one of the easiest and best ways to cook this healthful and delicious food.

The first rule in grilling fish and shellfish is to buy only the freshest available. How can you tell what's fresh? Whole fish should have shiny skin and bright eyes with clear, black—not cloudy—pupils. It should smell fresh, not fishy. Fillets and steaks should look moist, with no discoloration toward the edges. The shells of clams and oysters should be shut tight. Scallops should be pale, creamy white, with a fresh briny scent. No matter what type of fish or shellfish you choose, if it's truly fresh, you're already more than halfway to a wonderful meal.

Keep the fish refrigerated until about 30 minutes before grilling. It should be near room temperature when it goes on the grill. If the fish is to be marinated for longer than 30 minutes, begin marinating it in the refrigerator but take it out of the refrigerator—but not out of the marinade—about 30 minutes before grilling.

Because fish cooks so quickly, it is easy to overcook it. Nothing ruins a nice piece of fish like overcooking. Years ago, Canada's Department of Fisheries produced a small pamphlet on cooking fish that has since become a classic. In it, they suggest determining the cooking time for any fish (using any cooking method) by simply measuring the fish at its thickest part and then cooking it for 10 minutes per inch of thickness. A 1-inch-thick steak (or fillet, or whatever) would take 10 minutes to cook: 5 minutes per side. If you're scrupulous about following this timing method, you'll please everyone—even those who say American home cooks always overcook fish.

If your marinade contains an acid component, such as citrus juice or vinegar, limit the time you marinate fish to under 30 minutes; any longer and the acid will break down the texture of the flesh, making it too soft.

People on the cutting edge of cuisine may say that this method is too generalized (and results in cooking times that are too long), but it's a very reliable starting point until you've had a chance to determine your personal preferences and the nuances of your own gas grill. Because there are so many different models and types of grills out there, it is best to rely on your own good sense for judging doneness and to use the times given in each recipe as a rough guideline.

Fish is considered done when its flesh just begins to flake when probed with a fork. Another way to determine doneness is to peek and see if the flesh is uniformly opaque. Translucent flesh is generally undercooked, though some people prefer it that way—especially with fresh tuna. A large piece of fish or thick steak can be tested for doneness with an instant-read thermometer. Look for a minimum temperature of 140° F.

When it comes to grilling shellfish, remember that the meat is at its peak the instant it has turned opaque all the way through. Follow the times given in each recipe as a guideline, but use your judgement. The fastest way to ruin any shellfish is to overcook it.

Sometimes fish will stick to the grill; there are several ways to avoid the problem. First, always preheat the grill, as instructed in the recipes. Once the grill is hot, use your wire brush to clean it. Fish is less likely to stick to a clean, hot grill. Also, make sure to oil the fish, per the instructions in each recipe, just before you put it on the grill. Some cooks like to brush the grill surface lightly with oil before preheating. Since it's harder to clean the grill rack than a grill basket, I use a hinged wire grill basket, which I coat with nonstick cooking spray.

If the fish's skin is intact (which will help it retain its shape), put it on the grill skin side first. Plan on turning fish only once—halfway through the total cooking time.

Generally speaking, fish should be served hot off the grill—within seconds, if possible. So have all the accompaniments ready to go before putting the fish on the grill. Heated plates help keep the fish piping hot; slip the plates into a 250° F oven about 15 minutes before eating time, along with a platter to catch the fish immediately after grilling.

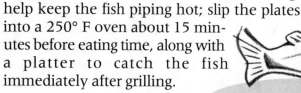

HALIBUT WITH
LEMON-CAPER BUTTER

F resh halibut is one of the finest fish there is for grilling: delicate, sweet, and moist. Unfortunately, the process of freezing and thawing halibut robs it of most of its moisture and delicacy, so stick to the fresh form, if at all possible.

LEMON-CAPER BUTTER
¼ pound butter
Juice of 1 lemon
1 teaspoon minced lemon zest (yellow part only)
3 tablespoons capers

4 halibut steaks or fillets, about 1½ to 2 pounds total,
  each about 1 inch thick
Vegetable oil
Paprika
Ground white pepper
Minced fresh parsley and lemon slices, for garnish
  (optional)

1. To make the lemon-caper butter, melt the butter in a small saucepan. Add the remaining lemon-caper butter ingredients, mix well, and set aside to cool completely.

2. Preheat the grill for 10 to 15 minutes, with all the burners on high.

3. While the grill is preheating, rinse the halibut in cold water and blot dry. Rub a little vegetable oil onto both sides of each steak or slice, and then dust with paprika and white pepper. Coat a hinged wire grill basket with nonstick cooking spray and place the halibut inside.

4. Once the grill is hot, turn all the burners to medium-high and cook the halibut for about 5 to 6 minutes per side, turning it once. The fish is done when it just begins to flake when probed with a fork.

5. To serve, whip the cooled lemon-caper butter with a fork. Place a couple of tablespoons of the butter on top of each piece of fish. Garnish with a sprinkling of parsley and a slice or two of lemon, if desired.

Serves 4

·◆· RED SNAPPER À LA VERA CRUZ ·◆·

This authentic recipe comes from friends who have spent a great deal of time in Mexico, traveling and sampling the cuisine from each region. This is how they serve red snapper in Vera Cruz.

VERA CRUZ SAUCE
2 tablespoons vegetable oil
1 large onion, chopped
3 garlic cloves, pressed
8 plum tomatoes, peeled, seeded, and chopped
4 to 6 tablespoons chopped canned jalapeño chiles
15 to 20 pitted green olives, halved
¼ teaspoon cinnamon
¼ teaspoon ground cloves
½ teaspoon sugar
Juice of ½ lemon
1 teaspoon salt

3 pounds red snapper fillets
Light vegetable oil, such as canola
Paprika
Ground white pepper
Chopped fresh cilantro and lemon wedges, for garnish
* (optional)*

1. To make the sauce, heat the oil in a medium-size saucepan. Add the onion and garlic and sauté until the vegetables are soft and transparent, but not browned—about 4 minutes. Add the remaining sauce ingredients and simmer, uncovered, for 5 to 10 minutes. Remove the pan from the heat and cover it until you are ready to serve the fish.

> *To avoid undue problems when turning fish on the grill, always place it perpendicular to the grill bars.*

2. Preheat the grill for 10 to 15 minutes, with all the burners on high.

3. While the grill is preheating, coat the red snapper fillets lightly with oil and then dust them with paprika and white pepper. Coat a hinged wire grill basket with nonstick cooking spray and place the fish inside.

4. Once the grill is hot, turn one burner off and turn the other(s) to medium. Position the snapper over the burner that is off, close the grill's lid, and cook for about 6 to 10 minutes for ½-inch to 1-inch fillets, turning them once. The fish is done when it just begins to flake when probed with a fork.

5. While the fish cooks, reheat the Vera Cruz sauce.

6. To serve, arrange the fish fillets on a heated serving platter and top with the sauce. Garnish with cilantro and lemon wedges, if desired.

Serves 6

•• ◆ ••

WHOLE SNAPPER WITH SPICY GINGER SAUCE

•• ◆ ••

Whole grilled fish are very impressive served hot off the fire. In this recipe, fresh small red snappers (about 2 pounds each) are first marinated in the clean, spicy flavors favored in Japanese cuisine, then grilled. The leftover marinade is heated and served as a dipping sauce. The dish is excellent served with steamed rice and steamed or sautéed bok choy (Chinese cabbage), dressed with a little rice wine vinegar and toasted sesame seeds.

MARINADE
¾ cup sake
¼ cup light vegetable oil, such as canola
¼ cup soy sauce
¼ cup grated fresh ginger
Juice of 1 lemon
2 large garlic cloves, pressed

1 teaspoon red pepper flakes

2 whole red snappers (about 2 pounds each), dressed
Chopped fresh cilantro, for garnish (optional)

1. Combine all the marinade ingredients in a shallow, non-reactive container and mix well.

2. Wash the snappers in cold water and blot dry. Using a sharp knife, cut diagonal slashes in both sides of the fish, as deep as the rib cage, but not through it or the backbone; this allows the marinade to penetrate the fish. Add the fish to the marinade, cover the container, and refrigerate for 1 to 2 hours.

3. Preheat the grill for 10 to 15 minutes, with all the burners on high.

4. While the grill is preheating, remove the red snappers from the marinade. Pour the marinade into a small saucepan. Coat a hinged wire grill basket with nonstick cooking spray and place the fish inside.

5. Once the grill is hot, turn one burner off and turn the other(s) to medium. Position the red snappers over the burner that is off, close the grill's lid, and cook for about 20 to 25 minutes, turning them once. The fish is done when the flesh is uniformly white and measures at least 140° F with an instant-read thermometer.

6. While the fish cooks, heat the leftover marinade just to the boiling point; reduce the heat to low, cover, and hold until ready to serve.

7. To serve, arrange the fish on a heated serving platter. Serve each person a portion of the fish and offer the bowl of heated marinade as a dipping sauce (chopsticks come in handy for this). Garnish the snapper with cilantro, if desired.

Serves 6

SALMON FILLETS WITH BLACK BEANS AND RED PEPPER PURÉE

The distinctive flavor of salmon stands up well to assertive foods, as witnessed in this recipe. Although the combination of salmon, black beans, and red peppers may sound a little questionable, wait until you try it! This is best served with a simple side dish, such as steamed white rice.

BEANS
15-ounce can black beans, drained and rinsed
½ cup minced onion
1 large garlic clove, pressed
1 cup chicken or vegetable stock
2 teaspoons chili powder
2 teaspoons ground cumin
1 teaspoon salt

RED PEPPER PURÉE
4 to 6 red peppers, roasted, peeled, seeded, and sliced
   (see page 187), or ¾ cup sliced roasted red peppers from
   a jar
2 tablespoons extra-virgin olive oil
1 teaspoon salt

4 salmon fillets, each about ⅓ pound to ½ pound
Vegetable oil
Paprika
Ground white pepper
½ cup sour cream or crème fraîche
Fresh cilantro leaves and lime wedges, for garnish

1. To make the black beans, combine all the ingredients in a pan. Bring to a boil and then simmer, covered, for 30 minutes, stirring occasionally. Allow the mixture to cool. Purée half the bean mixture in a blender or food processor. Return the purée to the pan and mix well. Adjust the seasonings to your taste. Keep the beans warm until serving time, adding a little more stock if the bean mixture becomes too thick (it should be thin enough to spoon onto a plate, but not runny).

2. To make the red pepper purée, place the peppers, olive oil, and salt in a blender or food processor. Purée until smooth. Transfer the mixture to a bowl until serving time.

3. Preheat the grill for 10 to 15 minutes, with all the burners on high.

4. While the grill is preheating, rinse the salmon fillets in cold water and blot them dry. Rub a little vegetable oil on both sides of the salmon and dust the fillets with paprika and white pepper. Coat a hinged wire grill basket with nonstick cooking spray and place the salmon fillets inside.

5. Once the grill is hot, turn one burner off and turn the other(s) to medium. Position the salmon fillets over the burner that is off, close the grill's lid, and cook the fish for about 5 minutes per side, turning them once. The fish is done when it just begins to flake when probed with a fork.

6. To serve, divide the black bean mixture among 4 prewarmed plates. Top each plate with a salmon fillet. Carefully spoon some red pepper purée over each fillet, then a little sour cream or crème fraîche. Garnish with the cilantro leaves and a couple of fresh lime wedges.

Serves 4

•◆•

SALMON STEAKS
WITH CUCUMBER-DILL SAUCE

•◆•

S almon combined with the flavors of cucumbers and dill is classic in the world of good eating. This dish is excellent served with Skewered Herbed Potatoes (page 191) and a green vegetable.

4 salmon steaks, each about 1 inch thick
Vegetable oil
Paprika
Ground white pepper

CUCUMBER-DILL SAUCE
¾ cup minced, peeled, and seeded cucumber
2 teaspoons dried dill weed or 1 tablespoon fresh dill

One-half pound
of fish is consid-
ered a good serv-
ing size for one
person.

½ *cup sour cream*
4 tablespoons butter, softened
1 teaspoon salt

1. Preheat the grill for 10 to 15 minutes, with all the burners on high.

2. While the grill is preheating, rinse the salmon steaks in cold water and blot them dry. Rub a little vegetable oil on both sides of the salmon and dust the steaks with paprika and white pepper. Coat a hinged wire grill basket with nonstick cooking spray and place the salmon steaks inside.

3. In a medium bowl, combine all the cucumber sauce ingredients and mix well with a fork. Keep the sauce at room temperature until the fish is ready. (If you make the sauce ahead of time, refrigerate it until about 30 minutes before serving time.)

4. Once the grill is hot, turn all the burners to medium-high. Grill the salmon steaks for about 5 to 6 minutes per side, turning them once. The fish is done when it just begins to flake when probed with a fork and measures at least 140° F with an instant-read thermometer.

5. To serve, dish out each salmon steak with a couple of tablespoons of the cucumber-dill sauce on top.

Serves 4

WHOLE GRILLED SALMON

Grilling a whole salmon is not for the faint of heart. To do it properly, you need your wits about you—and another person to help play "stereo" spatulas when it's time to turn the fish. That said, a whole salmon is one of the most impressive items to come off any grill. Serve with either the lemon beurre blanc from the next recipe or the cucumber-dill sauce from the previous recipe.

1 fresh whole salmon (about 5 to 6 pounds), dressed,
    with head and tail intact

1 or 2 fresh lemons, sliced thin
1 medium onion, sliced thin
3 or 4 celery tops, with leaves
Fresh dill (dried dill weed will do, if necessary)
Vegetable oil
Lemon wedges, for garnish

1. Preheat the grill for 10 to 15 minutes, with all the burners on high.

2. While the grill is preheating, rinse the salmon well with cold water and blot it dry. Layer the lemon and onion slices, celery tops, and dill evenly in the cavity of the fish. Sew the cavity shut with a large needle and white cotton thread, using the most rudimentary of stitches. If a needle and thread are not available, thread a couple of presoaked bamboo skewers across the opening to keep the stuffing from falling out. Rub some vegetable oil lightly on both sides of the fish.

3. Once the grill is hot, turn one burner off and turn the other(s) to medium. Position the salmon over the burner that is off, close the grill's lid, and cook the fish for about 40 to 60 minutes, or until a thermometer inserted into the flesh reads 140° F. Turn once, halfway through the cooking process: This is when two sets of hands and two spatulas come in very handy. Position the two spatulas under the salmon and roll it over gently.

4. When the fish is done, transfer it to a warm serving platter and garnish with the lemon wedges. To serve, use a very sharp, heavy knife to remove the head and tail, and then cut straight through the body of the fish crosswise, making individual salmon steaks.

Serves 10 to 12

◆

SEA BASS WITH
LEMON BEURRE BLANC

◆

Sea bass is a first-rate fish for grilling. Delicate in flavor and texture, it is beautifully complemented by the tangy richness of a beurre blanc. The very literal translation of *beurre blanc* is "white butter." Once you learn how to make beurre blanc, you'll return to it again and again when you need something special to transform a good dish into a great one.

It's best to make the beurre blanc before you grill the fish. To hold the sauce in the interim, you'll need a Thermos bottle large enough to contain about 1½ cups of the sauce. *Note:* You can modify this recipe very easily by adding 2 to 3 tablespoons of your favorite herb (such as basil, tarragon, or chervil), minced, to the shallot-and-vinegar mixture.

LEMON BEURRE BLANC
3 or 4 shallots, minced, or ¼ cup minced green onions
  (white parts only)
¼ cup white wine vinegar
¼ cup white wine (or for a more complex flavor, ¼ cup dry
  vermouth)
Juice of ½ lemon
½ teaspoon grated lemon zest (yellow part only)
1 cup butter, sliced into about 10 pats

4 fresh sea bass fillets, each about ⅓ pound to ½ pound
Vegetable oil
Ground white pepper
Lemon wedges and chopped fresh parsley, for garnish
  (optional)

1. To make the beurre blanc, put the shallots or onions, white wine vinegar, wine or vermouth, lemon juice, and lemon zest into a small saucepan and bring the mixture to a boil. Reduce the sauce rapidly over high heat until only 2 tablespoons of liquid remain. Watch carefully, and stir or swirl the mixture more or less constantly.

2. Reduce the heat to medium-low and begin adding the butter, one pat at a time, whisking constantly. Allow each pat of butter to dissolve almost completely before adding the next. By the time the last pat of butter has been added, the sauce should be thick and creamy. Pour the sauce into a preheated Thermos bottle to hold until serving time.

3. Preheat the grill for 10 to 15 minutes, with all the burners on high.

4. While the grill is preheating, rinse the sea bass fillets with cold water and blot them dry. Rub a little vegetable oil on both sides of each fillet and then dust each one with white pepper. Coat a hinged wire grill basket with nonstick cooking spray and place the fillets inside.

5. Once the grill is hot, turn all the burners to medium-high. Grill the sea bass for about 4 to 5 minutes per side, turning them once. The fish is done when it just begins to flake when probed with a fork.

6. To serve, pour a few tablespoons of the beurre blanc over each fillet, and garnish with lemon wedges and a little parsley, if desired.

Serves 4

⋆⋆◆⋆⋆

SHARK STEAKS WITH CHILI-LIME BUTTER

⋆⋆◆⋆⋆

As frightening as sharks may be in the briny deep, you definitely shouldn't shy away from them in the fish market. Your local fishmonger may sell both small sharks (as steaks) and large ones (in slices). All have a firm texture and a flavor similar to that of swordfish. Excellent side dishes to serve with this recipe include black beans and steamed rice, with a spicy, fresh salsa for the top of the fish.

CHILI-LIME BUTTER
¼ cup butter
3 tablespoons fresh lime juice
2 teaspoons chili powder
1 teaspoon minced lime peel (green part only)
Salt and fresh-ground black pepper to taste

4 shark steaks or pieces, each about 1 inch thick
Vegetable oil
Ground white pepper
Lime wedges and chopped fresh cilantro, for garnish
   (optional)

1. To make the chili-lime butter, melt the butter in a small

........◆........
The following five types of fish are the easiest to handle on the grill:
   Salmon
   Shark
   Swordfish
   Trout
   Tuna

saucepan. Remove the butter from the heat and let it cool partially. Add the rest of the chili-lime butter ingredients and mix well. Keep the butter warm to use as a sauce at serving time, or let it cool completely, to use as a topping for the grilled shark.

2. Preheat the grill for 10 to 15 minutes, with all the burners on high.

3. While the grill is preheating, rinse the shark steaks or pieces with cold water and blot them dry. Rub a little vegetable oil on both sides of each one and dust with white pepper. Coat a hinged wire grill basket with nonstick cooking spray and place the pieces inside.

4. Once the grill is hot, turn all the burners to medium-high. Grill the shark steaks for about 5 to 6 minutes per side, turning them once.

5. To serve, pour or spoon a few tablespoons of the chili-lime butter over each piece of shark. Garnish with lime wedges and a little cilantro, if desired.

Serves 4

•◆•

SWORDFISH STEAKS WITH SAUCE NIÇOISE

•◆•

With its firm, almost meatlike texture, swordfish is one of the easiest fish to cook on the grill—not to mention one of the tastiest. Swordfish has a distinctive flavor that stands up well to strong-flavored sauces and marinades. In this Mediterranean-style recipe, the sauce *niçoise* is redolent with the aromas of garlic, lemon, and anchovy.

SAUCE *NIÇOISE*
¼ pound butter
Juice of 1 lemon
2 garlic cloves, pressed
4 (or more) anchovy fillets, rinsed
2 tablespoons minced fresh parsley
1 teaspoon fresh-ground black pepper

4 *swordfish steaks (about 2 pounds), each about 1 inch*
   thick
Vegetable oil
Paprika
Ground white pepper
Minced fresh parsley and lemon slices, for garnish
   (optional)

1. To make the sauce *niçoise*, melt the butter in a small saucepan. Add the remaining sauce ingredients, using a fork or spoon to mash the anchovy into unrecognizable bits. (Even people who say they hate anchovies will like this sauce, as long as they can't see the anchovies.) Remove the sauce from the heat and let it cool completely.

2. Preheat the grill for 10 to 15 minutes, with all the burners on high.

3. While the grill is preheating, rinse the swordfish steaks with cold water and blot them dry. Rub a little vegetable oil on both sides of each steak and dust each one with paprika and white pepper. Coat a hinged wire grill basket with nonstick cooking spray and place the swordfish inside.

4. Once the grill is hot, turn all the burners to medium. Grill the swordfish for about 5 to 6 minutes per side, turning it once. The fish is done when its flesh is completely opaque and measures at least 140° F with an instant-read thermometer.

5. To serve, whip the sauce with a fork and place a few table-spoons of it on top of each piece of fish. Garnish with a sprinkling of parsley and a slice or two of lemon, if desired.

Serves 4

•◆•

SWORDFISH BROCHETTES WITH LEMON–WHITE WINE MARINADE

•◆•

The firm texture of swordfish makes it ideal for cooking on skewers. Serve these meaty nuggets with steamed rice and a steamed green vegetable for a healthy, satisfying meal.

MARINADE
⅔ cup dry white wine
Juice of 2 lemons
3 tablespoons extra-virgin olive oil
2 tablespoons minced onion
2 garlic cloves, pressed
¼ teaspoon salt
Fresh-ground black pepper to taste

1½ pounds to 2 pounds fresh swordfish steaks, cut into
 1¼-inch cubes
12 bamboo skewers, soaked in water

1. Combine all the marinade ingredients in a medium-size, nonreactive bowl and mix well. Rinse the swordfish cubes with cold water and blot them dry. Add the fish to the marinade, making sure that the marinade covers all the fish. Cover the bowl, and refrigerate for 45 to 60 minutes.

2. Preheat the grill for 10 to 15 minutes, with all the burners on high.

3. While the grill is preheating, drain off the marinade and discard it. Thread the cubes of swordfish on the skewers, with the sides just touching. Coat a hinged wire grill basket with nonstick cooking spray and place the swordfish brochettes inside.

4. Once the grill is hot, turn all the burners to medium. Grill the skewered swordfish for about 5 to 6 minutes per side, turning them once. The fish is done when the flesh is uniformly opaque.

5. Place the brochettes on a warm serving platter and serve at once.

Serves 4

MEDITERRANEAN SWORDFISH BROCHETTES

·•◆•·

The fresh-tasting marinade that flavors the swordfish in this recipe is complemented by a garnish of sliced black olives and chopped parsley.

MARINADE
⅔ cup dry white wine
Juice of 2 lemons
3 tablespoons extra-virgin olive oil
1 tablespoon soy sauce
½ teaspoon dried oregano, crumbled
Fresh-ground black pepper to taste

1½ pounds to 2 pounds fresh swordfish steaks, cut into
　1¼-inch cubes
12 bamboo skewers, soaked in water
Sliced black olives and minced fresh parsley, for garnish

1. Combine all the marinade ingredients in a medium-size, nonreactive bowl and mix well. Rinse the swordfish cubes with cold water and blot them dry. Add the swordfish to the marinade, making sure the marinade covers all the fish. Cover the bowl and refrigerate for 45 to 60 minutes.

2. Preheat the grill for 10 to 15 minutes, with all the burners on high.

3. While the grill is preheating, thread the cubes of swordfish onto the skewers, with the sides just touching. Coat a hinged wire grill basket with nonstick cooking spray and place the swordfish brochettes inside.

4. Once the grill is hot, turn all the burners to medium. Grill the skewered swordfish for about 5 to 6 minutes per side, turning them once. The fish is done when the flesh is uniformly opaque.

5. Place the swordfish brochettes on a prewarmed serving platter, garnish with the olives and parsley, and serve.

Serves 4

WHOLE "CAMP-STYLE" TROUT

Now that fresh farm-raised trout are so readily available in markets across the country, you needn't go camping to obtain and eat these delicacies. Even so, we all should continue to experience the wonderful aroma and flavor of trout wrapped in bacon, cooked over an open fire, whether in the wild or in our own backyards. Count on 1 trout per person.

4 whole trout, each 10 to 12 inches long, dressed
4 fresh thyme sprigs, or 1 teaspoon dried thyme leaves
4 bacon strips, partially cooked
Lemon wedges, for garnish

1. Preheat the grill for 10 to 15 minutes, with all the burners on high.

2. While the grill is preheating, rinse the trout well with cold water and blot them dry. Place 1 sprig of fresh thyme, or ¼ teaspoon dried thyme, in the cavity of each fish. Wrap each trout around the middle with a strip of partially cooked bacon; hold the bacon in place with toothpicks, if necessary. Coat a hinged wire grill basket with nonstick cooking spray and place the trout inside.

3. Once the grill is hot, turn one burner off and turn the other(s) to medium. Position the trout over the burner that is off, close the grill's lid, and cook for about 7 minutes per side, turning them once. When done, the fish will be opaque in the center and just begin to flake when probed with a fork.

4. Transfer the trout to a warm serving platter; discard the bacon. Garnish the fish with the lemon wedges and serve.

Serves 4

+◆+
FRESH TUNA WITH HOMEMADE TARTAR SAUCE
+◆+

If you're a little reluctant to cook fish on the grill, this recipe will win you over. Tuna, with its dense, firm texture, is probably the easiest of all fish to grill to perfection. Serve this dish with steamed rice or baked potatoes.

TARTAR SAUCE
½ cup mayonnaise
3 tablespoons Dijon mustard
3 tablespoons extra-virgin olive oil
1 tablespoon white wine vinegar or white cider vinegar
2 tablespoons minced green onion (white part only)
4 tablespoons minced sweet or sour pickles

4 fresh tuna steaks (about 2 pounds), each about 1 inch thick
Vegetable oil
Paprika
Ground white pepper
Lemon wedges and chopped fresh parsley, for garnish (optional)

1. Combine all the tartar sauce ingredients in a bowl and mix well. Refrigerate the tartar sauce until serving time.

2. Preheat the grill for 10 to 15 minutes, with all the burners on high.

3. While the grill is preheating, rinse the tuna steaks with cold water and blot them dry. Rub a little vegetable oil on both sides of each piece and dust each one with paprika and white pepper. Coat a hinged wire grill basket with nonstick cooking spray and place the tuna inside.

4. Once the grill is hot, turn all the burners to medium-high. Grill the tuna for about 5 to 6 minutes per side, turning them once. When the fish is cooked, it will be only slightly translucent in the center.

5. To serve, spoon a few tablespoons of the tartar sauce over each piece of tuna. Garnish with the lemon wedges and a little parsley, if desired.

Serves 4

··◆··

GRILLED TUNA
WITH TUSCAN WHITE BEANS

··◆··

This highly unlikely combination makes for a delicious warm-weather meal. All that's needed as an accompaniment is a loaf of crusty Italian bread and some chilled white wine. *Bellissimo!*

BEANS
3 tablespoons olive oil
1 medium onion, minced
*Two 15-ounce cans small white beans, drained and
    rinsed*
2 cups chicken or vegetable stock
2 to 3 large garlic cloves, pressed
2 bay leaves
2 teaspoons salt
2 teaspoons fresh-ground black pepper

DRESSING
1½ cups extra-virgin olive oil
½ cup red wine vinegar
½ cup fresh basil leaves
2 garlic cloves, pressed
4 tablespoons water
2 tablespoons Dijon mustard
1 teaspoon salt
2 teaspoons fresh-ground black pepper

4 tuna steaks (about 2 pounds), each about 1 inch thick
Vegetable oil
Ground white pepper

2 red-ripe tomatoes, cut into wedges
2 lemons, cut into wedges

2 to 3 tablespoons chopped fresh parsley
2 to 3 tablespoons chopped fresh basil

1. To make the beans, warm the oil in a large saucepan over medium heat. Add the onion and sauté until soft and transparent, about 3 minutes. Add the beans, stock, garlic, and seasonings. Bring the mixture to a boil and then simmer, uncovered, for 30 minutes, stirring occasionally. Remove the pan from the heat and allow the beans to cool to room temperature. Taste the beans, adjust the seasonings, and hold at room temperature until serving time.

2. To make the dressing, combine all the ingredients in a blender. Blend well and hold at room temperature until serving time.

3. Preheat the grill for 10 to 15 minutes, with all the burners on high.

4. While the grill is preheating, rinse the tuna with cold water and blot it dry. Rub a little vegetable oil on both sides of each piece and dust each one with white pepper. Coat a hinged wire grill basket with nonstick cooking spray and place the tuna inside.

5. Once the grill is hot, turn the burners to medium-high. Grill the tuna for about 5 minutes per side, turning it once. When done, the fish will be only slightly translucent in the center.

6. To serve, use a slotted spoon to place the white beans on a large serving platter. Break up the grilled tuna into chunks about 1½ to 2 inches in diameter. Pour the dressing over the tuna, spilling some dressing on the beans. (You may have more dressing than you need, but in this case it's better to have too much than too little—especially if there are any leftovers.) Garnish the platter with the tomatoes and lemons, and sprinkle the parsley and basil all over.

Serves 4 to 6

⋄◆⋄

SEARED TUNA STEAKS WITH MANGO SALSA

⋄◆⋄

Although this recipe calls for simply searing the tuna, leaving the interior quite "rare," feel free to cook the fish longer. The sprightly flavors of the mango salsa are an excellent match for the rich flavor of the tuna. Serve with steamed rice and sautéed Chinese cabbage splashed with a little rice vinegar.

MANGO SALSA

2 fresh, ripe mangoes, peeled and chopped into small cubes
½ cup minced red onion
2 tablespoons chopped canned jalapeño chiles
¼ cup minced fresh cilantro
2 tablespoons fresh (not bottled) lime juice

4 fresh tuna steaks (about 2 pounds), each about 1 inch thick
2 tablespoons vegetable oil
2 tablespoons mixed fresh-ground black, green, red, and white peppercorns

1 lime, cut into 4 wedges, for garnish

1. In a ceramic or glass bowl, combine all the salsa ingredients and mix well. Let the salsa sit at room temperature for at least 30 minutes, stirring it occasionally.

2. Preheat the grill for 10 to 15 minutes, with all the burners on high.

3. While the grill is preheating, rinse the tuna steaks with cold water and blot them dry. Place the tuna in a shallow dish and completely coat both sides of each piece with vegetable oil. Sprinkle each piece with the peppercorn mixture, pressing it slightly into the tuna.

4. Once the grill is hot, cook the tuna steaks directly over high heat for about 2 to 3 minutes per side, turning them once. This short cooking time will leave the interior of the fish "rare." For more well-done tuna, grill the steaks over medium-high heat for 5 minutes per side, turning them once.

5. Serve the fish with the mango salsa on the side and a wedge of lime.

Serves 4

✦ ✦ ✦
SEARED FRESH TUNA SALAD
✦ ✦ ✦

When fresh tuna is seared on the outside but still pink on the inside, it approximates the taste and texture of Japanese sashimi. This salad, which is an ideal luncheon dish, is at once light and pungent.

DRESSING
⅔ cup light vegetable oil, such as canola
⅓ cup rice wine vinegar
1 tablespoon soy sauce
Juice of ½ lemon
1 tablespoon grated fresh ginger
1 garlic clove, pressed

4 fresh tuna steaks (about 2 pounds), each about 1 inch
   thick
Vegetable oil
Ground white pepper

8 to 12 cups mixed salad greens
Green onions, sliced lengthwise, then cut into 2-inch
   pieces, for garnish

1. To make the dressing, combine all the ingredients in a blender. Blend well and reserve at room temperature.

2. Preheat the grill for 10 to 15 minutes, with all the burners on high.

3. While the grill is preheating, rinse the tuna steaks with cold water and blot them dry. Rub a little vegetable oil on both sides of each piece and dust with white pepper. Coat a hinged wire grill basket with nonstick cooking spray and place the tuna inside.

4. Divide the salad greens among 4 to 6 plates and set aside.

5. Once the grill is hot, cook the steaks directly over high heat for about 2 to 3 minutes per side, turning them once. This short cooking time will leave the interior of the fish "rare." For more well-done tuna, grill the steaks over medium-high heat for about 5 minutes per side, turning them once.

6. To serve, break up the tuna in chunks that are 1½ to 2 inches in diameter. Place equal portions of the tuna on top of the greens on each plate. Drizzle some of the dressing over each plate and garnish with the green onions. Pass additional dressing at the table.

Serves 4 to 6

◆

SALADE NIÇOISE
WITH FRESH GRILLED TUNA

◆

This salad from the Riviera is hearty enough to serve as a main course. Replacing the customary canned tuna with fresh grilled tuna dramatically improves this traditional recipe. You can grill the tuna ahead of time and simply refrigerate it until you are ready to assemble the salad.

VINAIGRETTE
¾ cup extra-virgin olive oil
¼ cup red wine vinegar
½ teaspoon Dijon mustard
1 tablespoon minced green onion
2 tablespoons minced fresh parsley
⅛ teaspoon salt
Fresh-ground black pepper to taste

4 fresh tuna steaks (1½ to 2 pounds), each about 1 inch thick
Fresh-ground black pepper

SALAD
About 6 cups lettuce greens
8 medium-size unpeeled new potatoes, scrubbed well
1½ pounds green beans, ends and strings removed
2 large tomatoes, cut into wedges
2 hard-cooked eggs, peeled and quartered
½ cup black olives (preferably the small niçoise *variety)*
1½ tablespoons capers
12 anchovy fillets, rinsed and drained (optional)

1. To make the vinaigrette, combine all the ingredients in a small, nonreactive bowl and mix well with a wire whisk. Refrigerate the dressing until serving time.

2. Preheat the grill for 10 to 15 minutes, with all the burners on high.

3. Rinse the tuna steaks with cold water and blot them dry. Brush each piece on both sides with olive oil, and sprinkle the tuna with pepper.

4. Wash and dry the lettuce greens and refrigerate them until serving time.

5. Once the grill is hot, turn all the burners to medium-high. Grill the tuna steaks for about 5 to 6 minutes per side, turning them once. When the steaks are done, transfer them to a plate, let them cool, cover them with plastic wrap, and refrigerate them until serving time.

6. Cook the potatoes in boiling salted water for about 15 minutes, or until the tip of a sharp knife easily penetrates the middle of the potatoes. Drain the potatoes and immediately plunge them into ice water to stop the cooking process. Drain the potatoes again, and then cut them into ¼-inch-thick slices. Pour enough of the vinaigrette dressing over the potatoes to coat them lightly. Refrigerate the potatoes until serving time.

7. Cook the green beans in boiling salted water until they are just tender, about 5 minutes. Drain the beans and immediately plunge them into ice water to stop the cooking process. Drain the beans again and refrigerate until serving time.

8. To assemble the salad, arrange the lettuce greens in an even layer on a large platter. Mound the potatoes, green beans, tomato wedges, and egg quarters evenly around the platter. Break up the grilled tuna steaks into good-size chunks and pile them in the center. Scatter the black olives and capers all over the salad, and garnish with anchovy fillets, if desired. Pour the remaining dressing over everything and let the guests help themselves.

Serves 4 generously

·◆· FRESH TUNA FISH SANDWICHES ·◆·

This may appear to be a common tuna sandwich: tuna fish, mayonnaise, mustard, lettuce, and bread. But all the ingredients have been cranked up a notch or two, transforming a simple meal into an uncommon delight.

½ cup mayonnaise
¼ cup Dijon mustard

Romaine lettuce leaves

1½ pounds to 2 pounds fresh tuna steaks, cut into 1¼-inch
  cubes
12 bamboo skewers, soaked in water
Vegetable oil
Paprika

Good quality, crusty Italian or French bread, cut into
  ¾-inch slices
Softened butter
Lemon wedges, for garnish (optional)

1. Combine the mayonnaise and Dijon mustard in a small bowl and mix well. Refrigerate the mustard sauce until needed.

2. Wash and dry the lettuce leaves and refrigerate them until needed.

3. Preheat the grill for 10 to 15 minutes, with all the burners on high.

4. While the grill is preheating, rinse the tuna cubes with cold water and blot them dry. Thread the cubes onto the skewers, brush them with vegetable oil, and sprinkle them with paprika.

5. Once the grill is hot, turn all the burners to medium-high. Grill the skewered tuna for about 5 minutes per side, turning them once. When done, the fish will be only slightly translucent in the center.

6. When the tuna is about 3 or 4 minutes away from being done, brush each slice of bread on both sides with the softened butter. Toast the bread on the grill for a minute or two on each side.

7. To assemble the sandwiches, put a lettuce leaf on each slice of toasted bread, pile the cubes of tuna on top of half the slices, add a dollop or two of the mustard sauce to the tuna, and cover with the remaining bread. Garnish the sandwiches with lemon wedges, if desired.

Serves 4 generously

·•◆•· FISH TACOS ·•◆•·

The very idea of tacos filled with fish may at first seem startling, but after your first bite, you'll understand. Although fish taco stands are just now making an appearance in the States, they've been popular in parts of Mexico forever.

COLESLAW
4 cups grated cabbage
1 apple (any variety), peeled and grated
1 onion, minced
½ cup mayonnaise
2 tablespoons fresh lemon juice
1 teaspoon ground cumin
Salt and fresh-ground black pepper to taste

MARINADE
¼ cup light vegetable oil, such as canola
Juice of 2 limes and 1 lemon
2 teaspoons crumbled fresh oregano leaves or 1 teaspoon
  dried oregano
1 teaspoon ground cumin
1 teaspoon salt
1 teaspoon fresh-ground black pepper

2 pounds mild white fish fillets, such as red snapper, cut
  into 1-inch-wide strips
12 bamboo skewers, soaked in water

8 corn tortillas
1 or 2 avocados, cut into slices
2 tomatoes, cut into thin wedges
Chopped fresh cilantro
Lime wedges
Salsa

1. To make the coleslaw, combine all the ingredients in a large bowl and mix well. Refrigerate the coleslaw until serving time.

2. Combine the marinade ingredients in a nonreactive container and mix well. Place the strips of fish in the marinade and set aside at room temperature for about 20 to 30 minutes. (Don't leave the fish in the marinade any longer, or the lime and lemon juices will "cook" the fish.)

3. Preheat the grill for 10 to 15 minutes, with all the burners on high.

4. While the grill is preheating, weave or thread the fish strips on the skewers. Coat a hinged wire grill basket with nonstick cooking spray and place the skewered fish inside.

5. Once the grill is hot, turn one burner off and turn the other(s) to medium. Position the skewered fish over the burner that is off, close the grill's lid, and cook the fish skewers for about 8 to 10 minutes, turning them once. While the fish cooks, wrap the tortillas in foil and place them on the grill next to the fish. They will be soft and warm by the time the fish is done.

6. To serve, place a couple of pieces of fish in each tortilla, along with some avocado slices, tomato wedges, and a little coleslaw. Top with some cilantro, a squeeze of lime, and a little of your favorite salsa.

Serves 4

> ....◆........
> *You can heat individual tortillas directly on the grill, with or without a little oil. If you're heating a large quantity of tortillas, wrap them tightly in a couple of layers of aluminum foil and place the packet away from direct heat on the grill.*

•◆•

GRILLED LOBSTER TAILS

•◆•

Those in the know say that the true flavor of lobster is achieved not by boiling or steaming but by grilling. The trick, as with all shellfish, is not to overcook it! You'll know the lobster is done the minute (the second, actually) the meat turns opaque white and the shell glows bright red. With lobster's distinctive taste, the only flavors most people want to add are a little melted butter and a squeeze or two of fresh lemon juice. If you're a fan of spicy foods, however, you may want to eschew the melted butter, as they do throughout most of the Caribbean, and try a little fresh lime juice and as much of your favorite bottled hot sauce as you like (any hot sauce made from habanero peppers is great with lobster).

4 lobster tails, each about ½ pound

½ cup butter, melted
2 lemons or 2 to 4 limes, cut in wedges
Your favorite bottled hot sauce

1. Preheat the grill for 10 to 15 minutes, with all the burners on high.

2. While the grill is preheating, wash the lobster tails with cold water and pat them dry. Using a sharp knife or a pair of kitchen shears, cut down the middle of the hard top shell and then bend the tail backwards to partially crack the back shell; this will prevent the lobster tails from curling while on the grill. Brush the lobster meat with some of the melted butter, reserving the rest.

3. Once the grill is hot, turn one burner off and turn the others to medium. Position the lobster tails over the burner that is off, close the grill's lid, and cook the tails for about 10 to 12 minutes total, turning them once. Remove the lobster tails from the grill as soon as the meat has turned opaque white and the shell is bright red.

4. Serve the lobster immediately with the melted butter, the lemon or lime wedges, and hot sauce.

Serves 4

•◆•

SCALLOP AND SALMON BROCHETTES

•◆•

This dish is not only one of the most beautiful things you can serve from the grill, but also one of the most delicious. Accompany the brochettes with one of the small pastas (such as *semi de melone*, or melon-seed pasta, which looks almost like rice when cooked), boiled in chicken stock and dressed with minced fresh parsley, a little olive oil, and some grated Parmesan cheese, along with Cherry Tomatoes en Brochette (page 199).

MARINADE
¾ cup dry white wine
⅓ cup light vegetable oil, such as canola
1 tablespoon minced shallot (or substitute the white part
    of a green onion)
1 garlic clove, pressed
Juice of ½ lemon
¼ teaspoon salt
1 tablespoon chopped fresh parsley

¾ pound sea scallops
¾ pound fresh salmon, cut into 1¼-inch cubes
12 bamboo skewers, soaked in water
2 teaspoons cornstarch
1 tablespoon soy sauce

1. Combine all the marinade ingredients in a nonreactive container and mix well.

2. Rinse the scallops and the salmon cubes with cold water and blot them dry. Submerge the scallops and salmon in the marinade and refrigerate for 1 hour or a little longer.

3. Preheat the grill for 10 to 15 minutes, with all the burners on high.

4. While the grill is preheating, drain the marinade and reserve it. Thread the scallops and the salmon alternately onto the skewers.

5. Place the cornstarch in a small bowl, add the soy sauce, and mix the two. Pour the reserved marinade into a small saucepan, stir in the cornstarch mixture, and bring to a boil for a minute or two. Remove the pan from the heat and allow the sauce to cool.

6. Once the grill is hot, turn one burner off and turn the other(s) to medium. Position the brochettes over the burner that is off, close the grill's lid, and cook for 8 to 10 minutes, turning the skewers once.

7. While the fish and shellfish cook, reheat the marinade.

8. To serve, transfer the scallop and salmon skewers to a pre-warmed platter and pass the sauce.

Serves 4

> *Food packed tightly on skewers will take longer to cook than food packed loosely.*

·◆·

SKEWERED SCALLOPS WITH BAY LEAVES

·◆·

Sweet and fine-textured, sea scallops are a true delicacy. As with any other shellfish, however, it is important not to overcook scallops: they go from tender to tough in seconds. The inspiration behind this pairing of scallops and bay leaves originally came from Julia Child.

1½ pounds sea scallops
12 bamboo skewers, soaked in water
About 18 bay leaves (cut in half if they are large)
½ cup butter, melted

2 or 3 lemons, cut in wedges, for garnish

1. Preheat the grill for 10 to 15 minutes, with all the burners on high.

2. While the grill is preheating, rinse the scallops with cold water and blot them as dry as you can. Thread the scallops onto the skewers, with the scallops' sides touching, placing a bay leaf between every second or third one. Brush the skewers liberally with some of the melted butter, reserving the rest.

3. Once the grill is hot, turn all the burners to medium-high. Grill the skewered scallops for about 2 to 3 minutes total, turning them once. Remove the scallops from the grill as soon as the meat has turned opaque white.

4. Serve immediately with melted butter and lemon wedges.

Serves 4

⋄⦁⋄

SKEWERED SCALLOPS WITH LEMON AND FRESH GINGER

⋄⦁⋄

Scallops simply refuse to put up with much fuss in the preparation department. If the sauce is too rich, or the cooking time is too long, the whole reason for serving scallops is lost. Here's a very simple recipe, just right for when the count around the table doesn't exceed four and you want to serve something special. Accompany the scallops with steamed white rice and sautéed Chinese cabbage doused with a little rice wine vinegar.

MARINADE/DIPPING SAUCE
⅔ cup sake
2 tablespoons light vegetable oil, such as canola
Juice of ½ lemon
1 tablespoon grated fresh ginger
1 garlic clove, pressed
¼ teaspoon salt
1 tablespoon soy sauce

1½ pounds sea scallops
12 bamboo skewers, soaked in water
Vegetable oil

1. To make the marinade, combine all the ingredients, except the soy sauce, in a nonreactive container and mix well.

2. Rinse the scallops with cold water and blot them as dry as you can. Submerge the scallops in the marinade and refrigerate for 45 to 60 minutes.

3. Preheat the grill for 10 to 15 minutes, with all the burners on high.

4. While the grill is preheating, drain the marinade and reserve it. Thread the scallops onto the skewers, with the scallops' sides touching. Brush the shellfish lightly with vegetable oil.

5. Pour the marinade into a small saucepan, add the soy sauce, and bring the mixture to a boil for a minute or two. Remove the pan from the heat and let the sauce cool.

6. Once the grill is hot, turn all the burners to medium-high. Grill the skewered scallops for about 2 to 3 minutes total, turning them once. Remove the scallops from the grill as soon as the meat has turned opaque white.

7. To serve, place the scallops on a prewarmed platter and pass the dipping sauce separately.

Serves 4

⋅⋅◆⋅⋅

GRILLED SHRIMP À LA SCAMPI

⋅⋅◆⋅⋅

Shrimp, lemon, butter, and garlic is a famous lineup. While the stovetop version is fairly rich, grilled shrimp—"scampi style"—is far less fattening but no less flavorful. Serve this dish with pasta tossed with a little olive oil, chopped fresh parsley, red pepper flakes, and grated Parmesan cheese.

MARINADE
½ cup extra-virgin olive oil
½ cup dry white wine
Juice of 1 lemon
3 to 4 large garlic cloves, pressed
2 tablespoons minced fresh parsley

2 pounds large shrimp, shelled, deveined, and rinsed
  with cold water
2 dozen bamboo skewers, soaked in water

1. To make the marinade, combine all the ingredients in a

nonreactive container and mix well. Add the shrimp and refrigerate for about 60 minutes.

2. Preheat the grill for 10 to 15 minutes, with all the burners
on high.

3. While the grill is preheating, pour off the marinade and
discard it. Thread the shrimp one at a time onto two parallel
skewers, to keep them from spinning around when you turn them
on the grill.

4. Once the grill is hot, turn all the burners to medium-high.
Grill the skewered shrimp for about 4 to 5 minutes total, turning
them once. Do not overcook the shrimp: they will be done just as
soon as they turn opaque throughout.

5. Serve immediately.

Serves 4

⋅⋄♦⋄⋅
BACON-WRAPPED
SPICY BARBECUED SHRIMP
⋅⋄♦⋄⋅

This recipe has quite an assortment of flavors: shrimp,
stuffed with a sliver of fresh jalapeño chile, wrapped in bacon, and basted with barbecue sauce. It's great for a midsum-
mer outdoor meal, served with steamed rice, a platter full of
sliced ripe tomatoes, and plenty of ice-cold beer.

*2 pounds large shrimp, shelled, deveined, rinsed with
cold water, and blotted dry*
*15 fresh jalapeño chiles, seeded and deveined, cut in
quarters lengthwise*
15 bacon slices, cut in half, partially cooked
12 bamboo skewers, soaked in water
Your favorite bottled tomato-based barbecue sauce

1. Cut a slit lengthwise about halfway through the back of
each shrimp. Insert a jalapeño quarter into the opening.

2. Wrap each chile-stuffed shrimp with a piece of bacon, and
then thread each nugget in turn onto two parallel skewers, to keep

the shrimp from spinning around when you turn them on the grill. Coat the nuggets liberally with the barbecue sauce.

3. Preheat the grill for 10 to 15 minutes, with all the burners on high.

4. Once the grill is hot, turn one burner off and turn the other(s) to medium. Position the shrimp skewers over the burner that is off, close the grill's lid, and cook for about 4 to 5 minutes total, turning the skewers once and basting them with additional barbecue sauce, if desired. Do not overcook the shrimp: they will be done just as soon as they turn opaque throughout.

5. Serve immediately.

Serves 4

◆

POULTRY AND GAME BIRDS

◆

CHAPTER THREE
POULTRY AND GAME BIRDS

·•◆•·

Today's "factory-farmed" poultry bear little resemblance to the barnyard fowl of yesterday, which were raised on what they could grub in the yard, supplemented with grains. And game birds, once the exclusive quarry of the hunters in the family, are now just another frozen food you can pick up at almost any supermarket. But what our modern birds lack in flavor, they compensate for in low cost and ready availability. And on the bright side, their blandness benefits from any number of seasonings and marinades.

Anyone who has ever eaten a piece of charred "barbecued" chicken that was still red at the bone knows that grilling chicken can be tricky. Not so with the gas grill. Bone-in poultry is ideal for cooking with indirect heat, something that a gas grill accommodates very well. After preheating the grill on high heat, simply reduce the heat to medium on one side and turn the other burner(s) off. Place the bird over the burner that is off, close the lid, and let the grill do its work. With indirect heat, there are no worries about flare-ups and unevenly cooked meat. If you place presoaked wood chips wrapped in a perforated aluminum foil packet over the burner that is on, you will get plenty of barbecue flavor.

FLATTENING THE BIRD FOR EVEN COOKING

.•◆•.

You'll get very good results with whole birds if you flatten them before grilling. By doing so, you create a piece of meat of uniform thickness that will cook more evenly. If you are going to marinate the bird, flatten it before putting it into the marinade. Here's how it's done.

1. Place the bird on a cutting board, breast side up. With a heavy chef's knife, cleaver, or pair of poultry shears, cut through the ribs on one side, as close to the backbone as possible. Make a second cut on the other side of the backbone, again as close to the backbone as possible. Remove the backbone completely.

2. Turn the bird breast side down and spread the rib cage apart. If you make a notch in the end of the breast bone near the wishbone, it will be easier to spread the rib cage.

........◆.........
Never remove the skin from a bird before grilling. The skin keeps the juices in and prevents the meat from drying out. After the meat is done, guests can remove the skin themselves, if they wish.

3. Turn the bird over and flatten it with the heel of your hand. In the process, expect some of the rib bones to break.

4. Make a slit in the bird's skin near the edge of each breast and tuck in the legs. Fold the wing tips under the wings. The bird is now ready for marinating or cooking.

MARINATING

‥◆‥

C hicken, which is plain-tasting otherwise, benefits a great deal from marinating, especially skinless, boneless breasts. Remember to combine marinade ingredients in a nonreactive bowl or baking dish, such as one made of glass, stainless steel, or ceramic. A zipper-lock plastic bag also works very well. Unless a recipe specifies a very brief period of marinating (less than 20 minutes), refrigerate the poultry in the marinade, taking it out of the refrigerator about 20 minutes before grilling.

JUDGING DONENESS

‥◆‥

P oultry should be cooked to medium, the point at which the juices near the joints run clear, instead of pink, after you insert the tip of a sharp knife into the thickest part of the meat. On a meat thermometer, the internal temperature will read between 170° F and 185° F. A whole bird will continue to cook a while after it is removed from the heat, so

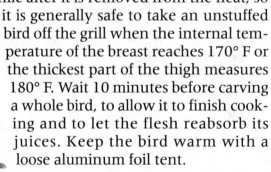

it is generally safe to take an unstuffed bird off the grill when the internal temperature of the breast reaches 170° F or the thickest part of the thigh measures 180° F. Wait 10 minutes before carving a whole bird, to allow it to finish cooking and to let the flesh reabsorb its juices. Keep the bird warm with a loose aluminum foil tent.

CHOOSING THE RIGHT BIRD FOR THE JOB

⋄◆⋄

CHICKEN

In general, the best chickens for the grill are the youngest. And, if you can find them, always favor a "free-range" chicken over a factory-raised bird: its superior flavor is worth the extra cost and shopping effort. Approximately 2½ to 3 pounds of dressed (bone-in) chicken feeds 4 people.

The youngest chickens are called "spring chickens" or "poussin." They are about 35 days old and weigh from 1 to 1½ pounds. They are excellent for the grill, especially when flattened. Broiler-fryers are young chickens, at least 45 days old, that weigh from 2½ to 5 pounds. They are also superb for the grill.

Beyond fryers are young roasters and stewing and baking hens, all of which need long, slow, moist cooking or stewing to tenderize their tough flesh. They are not generally recommended for grilling.

TURKEY

When shopping for a turkey, look for a bird that is broad and plump rather than tall and scrawny. As a general rule, hens are always favored over toms, and the hen's skin should be pearly white rather than bluish. Count on about 1 pound of whole, dressed turkey per person, which means that a 16-pound turkey will feed 16 people.

If the turkey comes with a thermometer in the breast, don't rely on it for grilling. Use your own meat thermometer, inserting it into the thickest part of the turkey thigh, where the thigh meets the body. The turkey will be done when the thermometer registers 180° F to 185° F. In a whole or half turkey breast, the internal temperature should reach 170° F.

ROCK CORNISH GAME HENS

Rock Cornish game hens are a cross between Cornish game cocks and White Rock hens. They are generally available only frozen and weigh between 1 and 1½

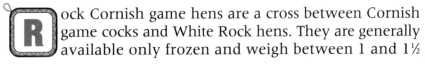

pounds. One game hen will feed one big eater, or two with more modest appetites.

Rock Cornish game hens are easiest to grill if they have been flattened first (see the preceding section, "Flattening the Bird for Even Cooking") and then marinated. Cornish game hens should be cooked to 170° F, at which point the juices run clear (instead of pink) when you insert the tip of a sharp knife into the thickest part of the thigh. If you are using a meat thermometer, that part of the thigh—where the thigh joins the body—is also where you should insert the thermometer.

QUAIL, DUCK, AND GOOSE

Unless you count some hunters in your circle of friends, you'll most likely find these game birds only in a supermarket freezer. All three are excellent cooked on the grill.

In general, these three game birds have richer, darker flesh than chicken: quail is the mildest and goose is the richest. Though most people prefer their poultry cooked well-done, there is a current trend to cook both quail and duck (especially the breast meat) only to the point where the meat is still translucent all the way to the bone.

POULTRY SAFETY

When it comes to poultry, especially thawing it and cleaning up after preparing it, a cliché says it best: better safe than sorry. Salmonella bacteria are killed at 140° F, so the real health risks come not with a bird cooked to 170° F, but at the beginning stages of preparing poultry.

Slow defrosting in the refrigerator is the preferred method with any frozen poultry. A frozen chicken may take 2 to 3 days to defrost, a turkey up to 3 to 4 days. All poultry should be thoroughly defrosted before cooking—make sure that there are no ice crystals in the cavity and no frozen areas in the breast meat.

Thoroughly rinse both defrosted and fresh poultry in water before cooking. After cutting or deboning, wash all utensils, including the cutting board and kitchen towels, in hot, soapy water.

Do not leave uncooked poultry—in marinade or not—out of the refrigerator for longer than 30 minutes before cooking.

Marinades used for raw poultry should never be reused, because blood from the raw meat will have leached into the marinade, posing a risk of salmonella poisoning. Before using the marinade as a basting sauce, bring it to a boil for several minutes to kill off any bacteria.

+◆+

WHOLE ROAST CHICKEN WITH LEMON AND GARLIC

+◆+

Some recipes follow the inverse rule of cooking: the simpler the recipe, the more flavorful are the results. Take this recipe, for example: it's simplicity itself, and yet the outcome is uniquely delicious. Once you try this method of roasting a chicken, you'll probably make it a staple in your culinary repertoire.

> *1 whole chicken, about 3 to 4 pounds*
> *1 whole lemon*
> *12 whole garlic cloves, peeled*
> *Extra-virgin olive oil*
> *Salt and fresh-ground black pepper*
> *Chopped fresh parsley and lemon wedges, for garnish*
>   *(optional)*

1. Wash the chicken inside and out with cold water, removing the excess fat, gizzards, heart, liver, and so on. Pat the bird dry. Using a skewer or a knitting needle, pierce the lemon several times all around and insert it into the cavity of the chicken. Arrange the garlic cloves around the lemon in the cavity. Force the wings of the chicken under the back to hold them in place. Using a piece of cotton string, tie the legs together tightly, gathering up the tail of the bird in between the two legs as you tighten the string. Rub the outside of the chicken with olive oil and dust with salt and pepper.

2. Preheat the grill for 10 to 15 minutes, with all the burners on high.

3. Once the grill is hot, turn one burner off and turn the other(s) to medium. Place the chicken breast side up over the burner that is off. Cook the chicken with the lid closed for 1¼ to 1¾ hours, or until a meat thermometer inserted into the middle of the breast registers 170° F.

4. When the bird is done, transfer the chicken to a serving platter and let it sit for 10 minutes before carving. Garnish each plate of sliced chicken with the parsley and lemon wedges, if desired, and serve.

Serves 4 to 6

WHOLE ROAST CHICKEN PROVENÇAL

A perfectly roasted chicken—skin brown and crisp on the outside, meat tender and moist on the inside—is one of the simplest and best meals ever devised. Though a whole chicken can be somewhat difficult to handle on the grill, a whole chicken that has been flattened is decidedly not. Flattening a chicken, or any poultry, from a quail to a turkey, is easy, as outlined on page 59. If you don't feel up to it yourself, ask your butcher to do it for you. This country meal is delicious served with White Onion Kebobs with Rosemary and Balsamic Vinegar (page 184) and grilled potatoes.

1 whole chicken, about 3 to 4 pounds

MARINADE
½ cup extra-virgin olive oil
¾ cup dry white wine
3 teaspoons herbes de Provence (available at most large
   supermarkets and specialty food shops)
Juice of 1 lemon
1 teaspoon salt
1 teaspoon fresh-ground black pepper

Chopped fresh parsley and lemon wedges, for garnish
   (optional)

1. Flatten the chicken according to the directions on page 59, or ask your butcher to do it for you. Wash the bird in cold water and pat it dry.

2. Combine all the marinade ingredients in a nonreactive container and mix well. Place the chicken in the marinade, cover the container, and refrigerate for 4 to 6 hours, or overnight if desired.

3. Preheat the grill for 10 to 15 minutes, with all the burners on high.

4. While the grill is preheating, drain the marinade from its container into a nonreactive saucepan. Bring the marinade to a boil, remove the pan from the heat, and reserve for basting.

5. Once the grill is hot, turn one burner off and turn the

other(s) to medium. Place the chicken, breast side up, over the burner that is off. Close the grill's lid and cook the chicken for 55 to 75 minutes. Turn the bird every 15 minutes, basting with the boiled marinade, if desired. The chicken is done when the juices run clear and a thermometer inserted into the breast reads 170° F.

6. When the bird is done, transfer the chicken to a serving platter and let it sit for 10 minutes before carving. Garnish each plate of sliced chicken with the parsley and lemon wedges, if desired, and serve.

Serves 4 to 6

••◆••

FLATTENED CHICKEN DIJONAISE

••◆••

Small, young chickens (around 2 to 2½ pounds) are perfect for this dish. Flattened chickens are not only easier to handle on the grill than unflattened ones, but also harder to under- or overcook than those cut in pieces. With the bones and skin intact, the end result is a more succulent, flavorful bird. Serve with Skewered Herbed Potatoes (page 191) and Grilled Whole Pesto Tomatoes (page 197).

2 small whole chickens, each about 2 to 2½ pounds

MARINADE
½ cup dry white wine or dry vermouth
⅓ cup extra-virgin olive oil
Juice of 1 lemon
2 to 3 garlic cloves, minced
3 tablespoons Dijon mustard
2 teaspoons fresh-ground black pepper

1. Flatten the chickens according to the directions on page 59, or ask your butcher to do it for you. Wash the birds inside and out and pat dry.

2. In a nonreactive container, mix together the marinade ingredients. Place the chickens in the marinade, turning them several times to coat them thoroughly. Cover the container and refrigerate for at least 1 hour.

3. Preheat the grill for 10 to 15 minutes, with all the burners on high.

4. Once the grill is hot, turn one burner off and turn the other(s) to medium. Drain the marinade from its container and discard it. Place the chickens, breast side up, over the burner that is off. Close the grill's lid and cook the birds for 35 to 45 minutes, turning them every 10 minutes or so. The chickens are done when the juices run clear and a thermometer inserted into the breast reads 170° F.

5. When the chickens are done, transfer them to a carving board and let them sit for 10 minutes. Use a sharp butcher knife or cleaver to cut each chicken along the breast bone into two equal halves. Serve hot off the grill or at room temperature.

Serves 4

··◆··

JAMAICAN JERKED CHICKEN

··◆··

Jamaican jerk is an intense seasoning: it's very spicy and usually very hot. It blends sweet spices, such as allspice and nutmeg, with fiery hot peppers. If your tastes run towards the exotic and you can stand the heat, this is a wonderful dish. Although you can find recipes for homemade Jamaican jerk seasoning, none quite compare to the marinades and rubs that are available in specialty food stores and through the mail. (One of my favorites is Walkerswood Jamaican Jerk Seasoning, from St. Ann, Jamaica, available via mail order from Le Saucier, Faneuil Hall Marketplace, Boston, Massachusetts 02109; 617-227-9649.)

1 cut-up chicken, about 3 to 4 pounds
Bottled Jamaican jerk seasoning rub or marinade
Vegetable oil (optional)

1. Wash the chicken parts in cold water and pat them dry. If you are using a dry jerk seasoning, mix it with the vegetable oil in a small bowl, according to the label directions, to make a paste-like marinade. Otherwise, use the marinade straight from the bottle.

The safest way to defrost any poultry is to allow it to thaw slowly and completely in the refrigerator.

Coat the chicken parts with the jerk seasoning paste or marinade, cover the pieces, and refrigerate for 1 to 3 hours.

2. Preheat the grill for 10 to 15 minutes, with all the burners on high.

3. Once the grill is hot, turn one burner off and turn the other(s) to medium. Place the chicken parts, skin side up, over the burner that is off. Close the grill's lid and cook the chicken for 45 to 60 minutes, turning the pieces every 15 minutes. The chicken is done when the juices run clear; the white meat will be done before the dark meat.

4. Serve the chicken hot off the grill.

Serves 4 to 6

OLD-FASHIONED BARBECUED CHICKEN

Sometimes we need to forget what's currently fashionable and return to a favorite meal from way back when. For many people, grilled chicken, with that wonderful, sticky, spicy, red barbecue sauce is one of those dishes. Served up with potato or macaroni salad and some sliced garden-fresh tomatoes—well, it's hard to beat. Even better, with a gas grill and the following instructions, you won't have to worry about burning the chicken the way your dad probably did.

1 cut-up chicken, about 3 to 4 pounds
Your favorite bottled tomato-based barbecue sauce

1. Wash the chicken parts in cold water and pat them dry. Pour a cup or so of the barbecue sauce into a nonreactive container, add the chicken, and turn the pieces to coat them well. Cover the container and refrigerate for 1 to 2 hours.

2. Preheat the grill for 10 to 15 minutes, with all the burners on high.

3. Once the grill is hot, turn one burner off and turn the

other(s) to medium. Place the chicken parts, skin side up, over the burner that is off. Close the grill's lid and cook the chicken for 45 to 60 minutes. Turn the pieces every 15 minutes, basting them with additional barbecue sauce if desired. The chicken is done when the juices run clear; the white meat will be done before the dark meat.

4. Serve the chicken hot off the grill, or let it cool, then refrigerate until needed. Remove from the refrigerator about 30 minutes before serving.

Serves 4 to 6

••◆••
TANDOORI CHICKEN
••◆••

The first time you make this traditional dish from India, you may wonder about the ingredients and doubt that the chicken will really turn out OK. Trust me, it will. A gas grill is particularly well-suited to preparing perfectly cooked tandoori chicken, without many of the burning problems associated with charcoal grills. Serve the chicken with steamed rice and perhaps Grilled Eggplant (page 177), doused with a little rice wine vinegar, and your favorite chutney.

1 cut-up chicken, about 3 to 4 pounds, skinned

MARINADE
2 cups plain yogurt
2 tablespoons grated fresh ginger
2 large garlic cloves, pressed
4 tablespoons vegetable oil (preferably peanut oil)
2 tablespoons paprika
1 tablespoon ground turmeric
2 teaspoons ground cumin
⅛ teaspoon cayenne, or more to taste
1 teaspoon salt

Chopped fresh cilantro, for garnish (optional)

1. Wash the chicken parts in cold water and pat them dry. Using a sharp knife, make diagonal slices about ¼ inch deep across each piece, to help the marinade penetrate the meat.

2. Combine all the marinade ingredients in a nonreactive container and mix well. Place the chicken in the marinade, cover the container, and refrigerate for 4 to 6 hours.

3. Preheat the grill for 10 to 15 minutes, with all the burners on high.

4. Once the grill is hot, turn one burner off and turn the other(s) to medium. Drain the marinade from its container and discard it. Place the chicken parts over the burner that is off. Close the grill's lid and cook the chicken pieces for 45 to 60 minutes, turning them every 15 minutes. The chicken is done when the juices run clear; the white meat will be done before the dark meat. Watch closely, because skinless meat will dry out if overcooked.

5. Transfer the chicken to a serving platter, garnish with cilantro, if desired, and serve.

Serves 4 to 6

SOUTHWESTERN CHICKEN

The flavors of the Southwest are authoritative and spicy, just right for chicken. Try combining this recipe with a side of Cowpoke Beans (page 224), steamed rice, and your favorite salsa.

1 cut-up chicken, about 3 to 4 pounds

MARINADE
¼ cup fresh lime juice
¼ cup apple juice
¼ cup vegetable oil
2 garlic cloves, pressed
2 teaspoons chili powder (hot or mild)

Chopped fresh cilantro, for garnish (optional)

1. Wash the chicken parts in cold water and pat them dry.

2. Combine all the marinade ingredients in a nonreactive container and mix well. Place the chicken in the marinade, cover the container, and refrigerate for 4 to 6 hours.

3. Preheat the grill for 10 to 15 minutes, with all the burners on high.

4. While the grill is preheating, drain the marinade from its container into a nonreactive saucepan. Bring the marinade to a boil, remove the pan from the heat, and reserve for basting.

5. Once the grill is hot, turn one burner off and the other(s) to medium. Place the chicken parts, skin side up, over the burner that is off. Close the grill's lid and cook the chicken pieces for 45 to 60 minutes, turning them every 15 minutes and basting them with the boiled marinade, if desired. The chicken is done when the juices run clear; the white meat will be done before the dark meat.

6. Transfer the chicken to a serving platter, garnish with cilantro, if desired, and serve.

Serves 4 to 6

Need a quick defrost method? Submerge the poultry in a large container of cold water. Allow 30 minutes of defrosting time for each pound, and change the water every 30 minutes.

•◆•

CHICKEN IN ZINFANDEL MARINADE WITH ONIONS AND MUSHROOMS

•◆•

This recipe for grilled, marinated chicken was inspired by the famous French country dish *coq au vin*. The hearty flavors are great for fall and winter dining. Serve with buttered, parslied noodles or brown rice and Garlicky Grilled Tomatoes (page 196).

1 cut-up chicken, about 3 to 4 pounds

ZINFANDEL MARINADE
¾ cup Zinfandel wine
3 tablespoons extra-virgin olive oil
2 garlic cloves, pressed
1 tablespoon Dijon mustard
½ teaspoon dried thyme leaves
¼ teaspoon fresh-ground black pepper

*1 pound whole white mushrooms, washed and stems
    trimmed*
1 pound whole small white boiling onions, peeled
2 dozen bamboo skewers, soaked in water

Chopped fresh parsley, for garnish (optional)

1. Wash the chicken parts in cold water and pat them dry.

2. Combine all the marinade ingredients in a nonreactive
container and mix well. Add the chicken, mushrooms, and onions,
cover the container, and refrigerate for 2 to 3 hours, or overnight.

3. Preheat the grill for 10 to 15 minutes, with all the burners
on high.

4. While the grill is preheating, drain the marinade from its
container and discard it. Thread the mushrooms onto one set of
skewers and the onions onto another.

5. Once the grill is hot, turn one burner off and turn the other(s)
to medium. Place the chicken parts, skin side up, and the skewered
mushrooms and onions over the burner that is off. Close the grill's lid
and cook the chicken and vegetables, turning the skewers after 5
minutes. The mushrooms will be done in 8 to 12 minutes, the onions
in 15 to 20 minutes. When the vegetables are done, remove them
from the grill and keep them warm. Continue to grill the chicken
pieces, for a total of 45 to 60 minutes, turning them every 15 minutes.
The chicken will be done when the juices run clear; the white meat
will be done before the dark meat.

6. Serve the chicken hot off the grill, along with the mushrooms
and onions. Garnish each serving with a little parsley, if desired.

Serves 4 to 6

•◆•
GRILLED CURRIED CHICKEN
•◆•

Using an intensely flavored dry rub, such as this curry combination, is a great way to flavor chicken in a hurry. The
taste will be improved if you rub the chicken parts with the

curry and then allow them to "marinate" in the refrigerator for a couple of hours before grilling.

1 cut-up chicken, about 3 to 4 pounds

CURRY DRY RUB
3 tablespoons prepared curry powder
1 teaspoon paprika
½ teaspoon ground white pepper
¼ teaspoon salt

Chopped fresh cilantro, for garnish (optional)
Chutney (optional)

1. Wash the chicken parts in cold water and pat them dry.

2. Combine all the dry rub ingredients in a large bowl and mix well. Cover the chicken parts with the curry dry rub. If time allows, refrigerate the coated chicken, covered with plastic wrap, for 1 to 2 hours.

3. Preheat the grill for 10 to 15 minutes, with all the burners on high.

4. Once the grill is hot, turn one burner off and turn the other(s) to medium. Place the chicken parts, skin side up, over the burner that is off. Close the grill's lid and cook the chicken pieces for 45 to 60 minutes, turning them every 15 minutes. The chicken is done when the juices run clear; the white meat will be done be-fore the dark meat.

5. Transfer the chicken to a serving platter and garnish with cilantro. Pass a jar of chutney at the table, if desired.

Serves 4 to 6

••◆••

CHICKEN DIJON

••◆••

Dijon marinade is an excellent complement to chicken—so much so that you may decide to make it a staple in your household. This chicken is great hot off the grill, or served at room temperature. Accompany with a cold pasta salad and a

simple salad of sliced tomatoes, peppers, and onions dressed with oil and vinegar.

1 cut-up chicken, about 3 to 4 pounds

MARINADE
½ cup dry white wine (or ½ cup dry vermouth, for a slightly stronger, more complex flavor)
⅓ cup extra-virgin olive oil
Juice of 1 lemon
2 to 3 garlic cloves, pressed
3 tablespoons Dijon mustard
1 teaspoon fresh-ground black pepper

Chopped fresh parsley and lemon wedges, for garnish (optional)

1. Wash the chicken parts in cold water and pat them dry.

2. Combine all the marinade ingredients in a nonreactive container and mix well. Place the chicken in the marinade, cover the container, and refrigerate for 2 to 3 hours, or overnight if desired.

3. Preheat the grill for 10 to 15 minutes, with all the burners on high.

4. While the grill is preheating, drain the marinade from its container into a nonreactive saucepan. Bring the liquid to a boil for a minute or two, remove the pan from the heat, and reserve for basting.

5. Once the grill is hot, turn one burner off and turn the other(s) to medium. Place the chicken parts, skin side up, over the burner that is off. Close the grill's lid and cook the chicken pieces for 45 to 60 minutes, turning them every 15 minutes, and basting with the boiled marinade, if desired. The chicken is done when the juices run clear; the white meat will be done before the dark meat.

6. Transfer the chicken to a serving platter, garnish with parsley and lemon wedges, if desired, and serve.

Serves 4 to 6

CHICKEN IN FRESH HERB MARINADE

If you have an herb garden, this dish is for you. Anytime from late summer to early fall, when the plants are in their full glory, pluck a handful of this and a handful of that. Serve the chicken with Rosemary Potato Wedges (page 192) and Mixed Vegetable Brochettes (page 203).

1 cut-up chicken, about 3 to 4 pounds

MARINADE
⅔ cup dry white wine (or ⅔ cup dry vermouth, for a
   slightly stronger, more complex flavor)
⅓ cup extra-virgin olive oil
Juice of 1 lemon
3 tablespoons chopped fresh basil
3 tablespoons chopped fresh parsley
1 teaspoon chopped fresh rosemary
1 teaspoon chopped fresh thyme
1 teaspoon fresh-ground black pepper

Lemon wedges, for garnish (optional)

1. Wash the chicken parts in cold water and pat them dry.

2. Combine all the marinade ingredients in a nonreactive container and mix well. Place the chicken in the marinade, cover the container, and refrigerate for 2 to 3 hours, or overnight if desired.

3. Preheat the grill for 10 to 15 minutes, with all the burners on high.

4. While the grill is preheating, drain the marinade from its container into a nonreactive saucepan. Bring the liquid to a boil for a minute or two, remove the pan from the heat, and reserve for basting.

5. Once the grill is hot, turn one burner off and turn the other(s) to medium. Place the chicken parts, skin side up, over the burner that is off. Close the grill's lid and cook the chicken pieces for 45 to 60 minutes, turning them every 15 minutes, and basting with the boiled marinade, if desired. The chicken is done when the juices run clear; the white meat will be done before the dark meat.

6. Transfer the chicken to a serving platter, garnish with lemon wedges, if desired, and serve.

Serves 4 to 6

••◆••
PESTO CHICKEN BREASTS
••◆••

Pesto, that legendary Italian concoction of basil, garlic, and pine nuts, imparts a wonderful, pungent flavor to chicken, especially when it is spread under the skin of the chicken breasts. Excellent ready-made pesto is available in your grocer's refrigerator case, or you can make your own using the recipe that follows.

PESTO
20 large basil leaves
2 garlic cloves, peeled
¼ teaspoon salt
1 tablespoon pine nuts, toasted lightly
2 tablespoons extra-virgin olive oil
3 tablespoons butter, softened
Fresh-ground black pepper

4 bone-in, skin-on chicken breast halves
Extra-virgin olive oil
Fresh-ground black pepper

1. To make the pesto, combine all the ingredients in a food processor and whirl until smooth or, for best results, mash them together with a mortar and pestle.

2. Preheat the grill for 10 to 15 minutes, with all the burners on high.

3. While the grill is preheating, wash the chicken breasts under cold water and pat them dry. Lift the skin from one end of a breast; using your fingers, separate the skin from the breast meat, but do not remove it. Spread a tablespoon or so of the pesto in an even layer between the skin and the meat. Repeat with the remaining breasts and pesto. Rub the outsides of the chicken breasts with olive oil and sprinkle them with pepper.

4. Once the grill is hot, turn one burner off and turn the other(s) to medium. Place the chicken breasts, skin side up, over the burner that is off. Close the grill's lid and cook the chicken for 25 to 35 minutes, turning the pieces every 15 minutes.

5. Serve the chicken hot off the grill.

Serves 4

CHICKEN BREASTS MARSALA

Marsala, a fortified wine from Sicily, may be somewhat out of favor these days, but its intense, semisweet flavor adds a unique dimension to this dish. For the best quality, look for wine labeled *Superiore*.

Although these chicken breasts serve only four people, adaptations of this and other chicken breast recipes are ideal for large buffet gatherings. Because chicken breasts are uniform in size and thickness, they all cook in about the same length of time.

4 bone-in, skin-on chicken breast halves

MARINADE
¾ cup Marsala wine
3 tablespoons extra-virgin olive oil
¼ teaspoon salt
¼ teaspoon fresh-ground black pepper

4 Swiss cheese slices
Chopped fresh parsley, for garnish (optional)

1. Wash the chicken breasts under cold water and pat them dry.

2. Combine the marinade ingredients in a nonreactive container and mix well. Add the chicken, cover the container, and refrigerate for 2 to 3 hours.

3. Preheat the grill for 10 to 15 minutes, with all the burners on high.

4. Once the grill is hot, turn one burner off and turn the other(s) to medium. Drain the marinade from its container and discard it. Place the chicken breasts, skin side up, over the burner that is off. Close the grill's lid and cook the chicken for 25 to 35 minutes, turning the breasts every 15 minutes.

5. About 10 minutes before the end of the cooking time, turn the breasts skin side up and top each one with a slice of Swiss cheese (folded in half, if necessary). Allow the cheese to melt and bubble slightly.

6. Serve the chicken hot off the grill, garnished with parsley, if desired.

Serves 4

••◆••

BONELESS CHICKEN BREASTS WITH FRESH HERB BUTTER

••◆••

With the recent interest in lighter cooking, boneless, skinless chicken breasts fit right in. They cook up in a flash on the grill and are easy to combine with other low-calorie, low-fat side dishes, such as steamed white rice and steamed vegetables. Of course, the fresh herb butter in this recipe contributes some fat, but you don't need to use much to add a lot of flavor.

FRESH HERB BUTTER
¼ cup butter, at room temperature
1 tablespoon fresh lemon juice
½ cup of a mixture of minced fresh basil, parsley, and chives

4 boneless, skinless chicken breast halves
Vegetable oil
Salt and fresh-ground black pepper

1. To make the fresh herb butter, combine all the ingredients in a small bowl and mix well with a fork. Let stand at room temperature for 1 hour.

2. Wash the chicken breasts in cold water and pat them dry. Rub each one with vegetable oil and them sprinkle on both sides with salt and pepper.

3. Preheat the grill for 10 to 15 minutes, with all the burners on high.

4. Once the grill is hot, turn one burner off and turn the other(s) to medium. Place the chicken breasts over the burner that is off. Close the grill's lid and cook the chicken for 10 to 12 minutes, turning once, just until the meat is opaque white all the way through.

5. Transfer the chicken to a serving platter, spoon a dollop of fresh herb butter on top of each breast, and serve.

Serves 4

◆

GRILLED CHICKEN FAJITAS

◆

Not that long ago, fajitas were fairly exotic fare. Today, after being popularized by so many restaurants, fajitas have found their way into many a home cook's repertoire—and for good reason: they're delicious, they're relatively low in fat, and everyone, including kids, seems to love them.

6 boneless, skinless chicken breast halves

MARINADE
½ cup vegetable oil
½ cup beer
Juice of 2 limes
2 garlic cloves, pressed
¼ cup chopped onion
1 tablespoon chili powder
2 teaspoons ground cumin
1 teaspoon ground oregano
1 teaspoon salt

Preheating the grill before you begin cooking helps ensure that food won't stick to the grill.

1 teaspoon fresh-ground black pepper

6 flour tortillas
3 green bell peppers
Tomato slices
Diced red onion
Avocado slices (optional)
Chopped fresh cilantro
Salsa

1. Wash the chicken breasts in cold water and pat them dry.

2. Combine all the marinade ingredients in a nonreactive container and mix well. Add the chicken, cover the container, and refrigerate for 2 to 4 hours.

3. Preheat the grill for 10 to 15 minutes, with all the burners on high.

4. While the grill is preheating, drain the marinade from its container into a nonreactive saucepan. Bring the liquid to a boil, remove the pan from the heat, and reserve for basting.

5. Once the grill is hot, turn one burner off and turn the other(s) to medium. Place the chicken breasts over the burner that is off. Wrap the tortillas in foil and put them on the grill next to the chicken, along with the whole bell peppers. Close the grill's lid and cook the chicken for 10 to 15 minutes, or until the meat is opaque white all the way through. Turn the pieces once during the cooking process and baste them with the boiled marinade, if desired.

6. To serve, cut the chicken into thin slices and place them on the warm tortillas. Remove the stems and seeds from the peppers, and slice them into thin strips. Top the chicken with the tomato slices, red onion, pepper strips, avocado slices, cilantro, and your favorite salsa or hot sauce.

Serves 6

SKEWERED CHICKEN TERIYAKI

Chicken teriyaki is an old standby. Whether you soak the chicken in the marinade given here or in one of the excellent bottled teriyaki sauces available today, nothing tastes like good old chicken-on-a-stick.

TERIYAKI MARINADE
½ cup soy sauce
⅓ cup dry sherry
¼ cup firmly packed brown sugar
¼ cup rice wine vinegar
4 tablespoons vegetable oil
2 garlic cloves, pressed
1 tablespoon ground dried ginger

6 boneless, skinless chicken breast halves
2 dozen bamboo skewers, soaked in water

1. Combine all the marinade ingredients in a nonreactive saucepan, mix well, and heat just to the boiling point. Remove the pan from the heat and let the sauce cool to room temperature. Transfer the marinade to a nonreactive container.

2. Wash the chicken breasts in cold water and pat them dry. Cut each half lengthwise into ½-inch strips. Place the chicken strips in the marinade, cover the container, and refrigerate for 1 to 2 hours.

3. Preheat the grill for 10 to 15 minutes, with all the burners on high.

4. While the grill is preheating, drain the marinade from its container and discard it. Thread the chicken strips onto the skewers so that the strips stay relatively flat.

5. Once the grill is hot, turn all the burners to medium. Grill the skewered chicken for 8 to 10 minutes, turning the skewers once.

6. Serve the chicken hot off the grill.

Serves 6

..◆..

SPICY CHICKEN THIGHS

..◆..

Among poultry lovers, chicken thighs have a bit of a cult following. Aficionados praise the thigh's succulence and meatiness, declaring it "the only part of the chicken really worth eating." Luckily for these folks, chicken thighs now come in their own packages. In this recipe, the thighs' flavorful meat is complemented by a complex and spicy marinade.

3 to 4 pounds skin-on chicken thighs

MARINADE
⅓ cup fresh lime juice
⅓ cup apple juice
3 tablespoons vegetable oil
2 garlic cloves, pressed
2 teaspoons chili powder
1 teaspoon hot pepper sauce

1. Wash the chicken thighs in cold water and pat them dry.

2. Combine all the marinade ingredients in a nonreactive container and mix well. Add the chicken, cover the container, and refrigerate for 2 to 3 hours, or overnight if desired.

3. Preheat the grill for 10 to 15 minutes, with all the burners on high.

4. While the grill is preheating, drain the marinade from its container into a nonreactive saucepan. Bring the liquid to a boil for a minute or two, remove the pan from the heat, and reserve for basting.

5. Once the grill is hot, turn one burner off and turn the other(s) to medium. Place the chicken thighs, skin side up, over the burner that is off. Close the grill's lid and cook the chicken for 40 to 60 minutes, turning the meat every 15 minutes and basting with the boiled marinade, if desired.

6. Serve the chicken hot off the grill.

Serves 4 to 6

HOT AND SPICY
CHINESE CHICKEN WINGS

In Hawaii, hors d'oeuvres are known as "puu-puus." There are puu-puus, and there are "heavy puu-puus." A heavy puu-puu is any food substantial enough to qualify as a main dish. These wings fit in the heavy puu-puu category, and they are wonderful served with steamed rice.

2 to 2½ pounds chicken wings

MARINADE
½ cup soy sauce
¼ cup hoisin sauce
¼ cup white vinegar
¼ cup honey
¼ cup pineapple juice
2 garlic cloves, pressed
¼ teaspoon red pepper flakes
3 tablespoons peanut or vegetable oil

Sesame seeds and chopped fresh cilantro, for garnish
*   (optional)*

1. Wash the chicken wings in cold water and pat them dry. With a sharp knife, trim off each wing tip right at the joint.

2. Combine all the marinade ingredients in a nonreactive container and mix well. Add the wings, cover the container, and refrigerate for 4 to 6 hours, or overnight if desired.

3. Preheat the grill for 10 to 15 minutes, with all the burners on high.

4. While the grill is preheating, drain the marinade from its container into a nonreactive saucepan. Bring the liquid to a boil for a minute or two, remove the pan from the heat, and reserve for basting.

5. Once the grill is hot, turn one burner off and turn the other(s) to medium. Place the chicken wings over the burner that is off. Close the grill's lid and cook the chicken for 30 to 35 minutes, or until the skin is crispy and brown. Turn the wings once during the cooking process, basting with the boiled marinade, if desired.

6. Transfer the chicken to a serving platter, garnish with sesame seeds and cilantro, if desired, and serve.

Serves 3 to 4

If you're going to use any leftover marinade as a baste or sauce for grilled food, be sure to boil it for several minutes first.

··◆··
CHICKEN BURGERS
··◆··

Now that ground poultry is easy to find in most super-markets, making chicken or turkey burgers at home is easy. For an added taste treat, be sure to toast the buns (lightly buttered first) on the grill while you cook the burgers.

1 pound ground chicken
4 tablespoons heavy cream
1 teaspoon salt
1 teaspoon ground white pepper
1 teaspoon seasoned salt
4 tablespoons butter, melted and cooled slightly
4 hamburger buns

1. Preheat the grill for 10 to 15 minutes, with all the burners on high.

2. While the grill is preheating, mix the ground chicken, cream, salt, pepper, and seasoned salt in a bowl. Because the ground chicken is very sticky, put a little of the melted butter on your hands and then shape the mixture into 4 patties, each about ½ inch thick. Place the patties on a ceramic plate and brush each one on both sides with some of the melted butter. The patties can be refrigerated up to 4 hours ahead of cooking time.

3. Once the grill is hot, turn all the burners to medium-high. Grill the chicken patties for about 15 to 18 minutes, turning them once.

4. A few minutes before the patties are done, brush the insides of the buns with the remaining melted butter, and toast them on the grill. Serve the patties in the toasted buns.

Serves 4

⁺⁺◆⁺⁺
WHOLE ROAST TURKEY
⁺⁺◆⁺⁺

There's no need to take up room in the oven when you can use your gas grill to roast a whole turkey to perfection. For this recipe, you'll need a disposable aluminum roasting pan large enough to hold the turkey.

1 whole turkey, about 10 to 12 pounds, fresh or thawed
2 teaspoons poultry seasoning
Vegetable oil
Salt and fresh-ground black pepper

1. Preheat the grill for 10 to 15 minutes, with all the burners on high.

2. While the grill is preheating, rinse the turkey inside and out with cold water, removing the neck, giblets, and any excess fat from the cavity. Pat the bird dry.

3. Dust the cavity of the turkey with the poultry seasoning. Rub the outside of the turkey with vegetable oil, and then sprinkle it with salt and pepper. Pull the skin over the breast cavity and fasten below (on the back) with a skewer. Force the ends of the wings under the back to hold them in position and then, using a piece of cotton string, tie the legs together, with the tail end securely in between.

4. Once the grill is hot, turn one burner off and turn the other(s) to medium. Place a roasting rack (if you have one) in the aluminum roasting pan and the turkey on the roasting rack. Position the turkey, breast side up, in the pan over the burner that is off. Close the grill's lid and cook the turkey for about 2 to 3 hours. About 30 minutes before the turkey is due to be done, remove the bird from the roasting pan, cut the string holding the legs together, and position the bird directly on the cooking grill (this allows for more even browning). Grill on both sides, about 15 minutes per side. The turkey will be done when a thermometer inserted in the thickest part of the thigh registers 170° F to 180° F. Save the drippings in the roasting pan for gravy.

5. Transfer the turkey to a carving board. Cover the bird loosely with a foil tent and let it rest for 10 to 15 minutes.

6. To carve the turkey, start on one side. First cut the leg and thigh sections completely off, then do the same with the wings.

Slice the breast meat thin, then cut the meat from the legs, thighs, and wings. Repeat on the other side. Serve immediately.

Serves 10 to 14

•◆•

FLATTENED TURKEY WITH SAUSAGE

•◆•

Flattening a turkey before you grill it is somewhat unusual, but it results in an incredibly moist and flavorful bird. Another uncommon technique, cooking the bird with sausage stuffed under its skin, actually improves the taste of both meats: the turkey picks up subtleties from the sausage, and the sausage absorbs flavors from the turkey.

> *1 whole turkey, about 10 to 12 pounds, fresh or thawed*
> *About 3 pounds bulk pork sausage*
> *Vegetable oil*
> *Salt and fresh-ground black pepper*

1. Flatten the turkey according to the directions on page 59, or ask your butcher to do it for you. Wash the bird in cold water and pat it dry. Remove the lumps of fat from inside the rib cage.

2. Using your fingers, lift up on the turkey skin, starting at the neck end, and separate the skin from the meat as completely as possible without tearing the skin. Push the sausage under the skin, making an even layer about ½ inch thick, over the breast, thighs, and legs, if possible, using as much sausage as you can. Smooth out the sausage layer by patting the turkey skin all over. Rub the turkey with vegetable oil and sprinkle it with salt and pepper.

3. Preheat the grill for 10 to 15 minutes, with all the burners on high.

4. Once the grill is hot, turn one burner off and turn the other(s) to medium. Place the turkey, skin side up, over the burner that is off. Close the grill's lid and cook the turkey for 1½ to 2 hours, turning it several times. The turkey is done when a meat thermometer stuck into the thickest part of the breast registers 170° F.

5. Transfer the turkey to a carving board. Cover the bird loosely with a foil tent and let it rest for 10 to 15 minutes.

6. To carve the turkey, start on one side. First cut the leg and thigh sections completely off, then do the same with the wings. Slice the breast meat thin, then cut the meat from the legs, thighs, and wings. Repeat on the other side. Serve immediately.

Serves 12 to 16

MEXICAN FIESTA TURKEY

T he idea for butterflying a turkey, soaking it in a Mexican-style marinade, and grilling it originated in *Sunset* magazine some years back. The recipe has gone through a few permutations since that time and has become a favorite of all who have tried it. This is wonderful party food: tasty, inexpensive, and festive.

1 whole turkey, about 10 to 12 pounds, fresh or thawed

MARINADE
¾ cup vegetable oil
¾ cup pineapple juice
½ cup fresh lime juice
2 teaspoons chili powder (hot or mild)
2 teaspoons dried oregano leaves, crumbled
1 teaspoon salt

Lime wedges and chopped fresh cilantro, for garnish
  (optional)

1. Flatten the turkey according to the directions on page 59, or ask your butcher to do it for you. Wash the turkey in cold water and blot it dry. Remove the lumps of fat from inside the rib cage.

2. Combine all the marinade ingredients in a very large zipper-lock plastic bag or other food-safe plastic bag and mix well. Place the turkey in the bag, seal it, and turn the bag a few times to coat the turkey with the marinade. Refrigerate for 4 to 6 hours or longer, preferably overnight.

3. Preheat the grill for 10 to 15 minutes, with all the burners on high.

Flattening poultry prior to grilling makes it much easier to handle on the grill, with no sacrifice in flavor or succulence. (See the instructions at the beginning of this chapter.)

4. Once the grill is hot, turn one burner off and turn the other(s) to medium. Drain the marinade from the bag and discard it. Place the turkey over the burner that is off. Close the grill's lid and cook the turkey for 1½ to 2 hours, turning it several times. The turkey is done when a meat thermometer stuck into the thickest part of the breast registers 170° F.

5. Transfer the turkey to a carving board. Cover the bird loosely with a foil tent and let it rest for 10 to 15 minutes.

6. To carve the turkey, start on one side. First cut the leg and thigh sections completely off, then do the same with the wings. Slice the breast meat thin, then cut the meat from the legs, thighs, and wings. Repeat on the other side. Garnish with lime wedges and cilantro, if desired, and serve immediately.

Serves 10 to 14

⁺⬦⁺

TERIYAKI TURKEY BREAST

⁺⬦⁺

Although you can use a boneless turkey breast for this recipe (which will shorten the cooking time slightly), a bone-in breast will turn out more flavorful and succulent. Feel free to substitute your favorite bottled teriyaki sauce for the recipe given here.

TERIYAKI MARINADE
½ cup soy sauce
⅓ cup dry sherry
¼ cup firmly packed brown sugar
¼ cup rice wine vinegar
4 tablespoons vegetable oil
2 garlic cloves, pressed
1 tablespoon ground dried ginger

1 whole bone-in turkey breast, about 5 to 8 pounds

1. Combine all the marinade ingredients in a nonreactive saucepan, mix well, and heat just to the boiling point. Remove the pan from the heat and let the sauce cool to room temperature. Transfer the marinade to a nonreactive container.

2. Wash the turkey breast in cold water and pat it dry. Place the turkey in the marinade, cover the container, and refrigerate for 2 to 3 hours, or overnight if desired.

3. Preheat the grill for 10 to 15 minutes, with all the burners on high.

4. Once the grill is hot, turn one burner off and turn the other(s) to medium. Drain the marinade from its container and discard it. Place the turkey breast over the burner that is off. Close the grill's lid and cook the turkey for about 1½ to 2 hours, depending on the size of the breast. Turn the turkey several times during the cooking process. The turkey is done when a meat thermometer stuck into the middle of the breast reads 170° F.

5. Transfer the turkey to a carving board. Cover it loosely with a foil tent, and let it rest for 10 to 15 minutes.

6. Carve the breast in thin slices and serve the turkey warm or at room temperature.

Serves 6 to 8

TURKEY TONNATO

One has to be an adventurous cook to try this dish because, let's face it, at first glance the ingredients for the *tonnato* sauce—a variation on a recipe developed by the late Michael Field—seem highly suspicious. Rest assured, however, that this is a tried-and-true recipe and a real crowd pleaser as well. An adaptation of the legendary Italian *vitello tonnato* (made with veal instead of turkey), this dish is superb served with crusty garlic bread and a fresh green salad—just the thing for a warm-weather al fresco luncheon or dinner.

1 whole bone-in turkey breast, about 5 to 8 pounds
Olive oil

TONNATO SAUCE
¾ cup extra-virgin olive oil
1 egg yolk

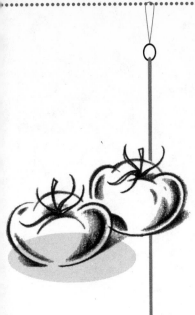

3-ounce can Italian oil-packed tuna (or domestic oil-packed tuna), drained
3 to 4 anchovy fillets, cut into small pieces
Juice of 1 lemon
⅛ teaspoon cayenne
¼ cup heavy cream
¼ cup chicken stock
2 tablespoons capers, rinsed in cold water and drained

2 tablespoons minced fresh parsley
1 bunch green onions, sliced thin
4 medium tomatoes, cut in wedges
2 lemons, cut in wedges
2 hard-cooked eggs, cut in thin rounds
½ cup small black or green olives (such as niçoise*)*

1. Preheat the grill for 10 to 15 minutes, with all the burners on high.

2. While the grill is preheating, wash the turkey breast in cold water, pat it dry, and rub olive oil all over it.

3. Once the grill is hot, turn one burner off and turn the other(s) to medium. Place the turkey breast over the burner that is off. Close the grill's lid and cook the turkey for about 1½ to 2 hours, depending on the size of the breast. Turn the turkey several times during the cooking process. The turkey is done when a meat thermometer stuck into the middle of the breast reads 170° F.

4. Transfer the turkey to a carving board and let it cool slightly. When the turkey is cool to the touch, remove all the bones, which will cut away easily, and skin the breast. Let the meat finish cooling, then wrap the turkey breast tightly in plastic wrap and refrigerate until needed.

5. To make the *tonnato* sauce, combine the olive oil, egg yolk, tuna fish, anchovies, lemon juice, and cayenne in a blender. Process by pulsing the motor on and off for no longer than it takes to produce a smooth purée.

6. Pour the purée into a bowl and stir in the cream. Add enough chicken stock to produce a sauce with the consistency of unwhipped heavy cream. Finally, mix in the capers.

7. Remove the turkey breast from the refrigerator. Using a large, sharp knife, cut the breast into ¼-inch slices.

8. Spread a thin layer of the *tonnato* sauce on a large serving platter. Arrange a single layer of the sliced turkey, slightly overlapping, on top of the sauce. Top with another thin layer of sauce. Continue alternating the turkey slices with the sauce until all the turkey has been coated. Immediately cover the platter tightly with plastic wrap, and refrigerate for 2 to 3 hours, or overnight.

9. About an hour before serving time, remove the platter from the refrigerator and let it come just to room temperature (if you serve the dish too cold, the flavors will be masked). On a fresh platter, gently fold each slice of turkey over itself, arranging the slices in an overlapping fashion. Top the meat with any sauce that remains on the original platter, garnish with parsley, green onions, tomatoes, lemons, hard-cooked egg slices, and olives, and serve.

Serves 8 to 12

Once the food has gone on the grill, it's a good idea to stick around and watch it cook. An unattended grill is an invitation to an overcooked dish.

❖
TURKEY BROCHETTES WITH PROSCIUTTO
❖

This recipe is an adaptation of the renowned Italian veal scaloppine Marsala with prosciutto. The turkey is an excellent (and much less expensive) substitute for the veal, and cooking it on skewers cuts the preparation time way down. If you can't find dry Marsala wine, substitute a medium-dry sherry.

> *1 boneless, skinless turkey breast half, about 3 to 3½*
> *pounds*
> *½ pound prosciutto, sliced very thin*
> *12 bamboo skewers, soaked in water*
> *Extra-virgin olive oil*
>
> MARSALA SAUCE
> *½ cup Marsala wine (preferably one marked* **Superiore***)*
> *½ cup chicken stock*
> *2 tablespoons butter, softened*
> *1 tablespoon minced fresh parsley*

1. Dice the turkey into 1¼-inch cubes. Cut the prosciutto slices in half. Wrap each turkey cube with a half slice of prosciutto. When all the turkey has been wrapped with the ham, thread the nuggets onto the skewers. Rub the brochettes lightly with olive oil.

2. Preheat the grill for 10 to 15 minutes, with all the burners on high.

3. While the grill is preheating, combine the Marsala wine, chicken stock, and butter in a small pan. Bring the mixture just to a boil, reduce the heat, and simmer, uncovered, for 10 minutes. Remove from the heat and reserve.

4. Once the grill is hot, turn all the burners to medium. Grill the skewers for 15 to 18 minutes, turning them once or twice.

5. Transfer the brochettes to a warm serving platter. Reheat the Marsala sauce, adding the parsley at the last minute. Pour the hot sauce over the turkey-prosciutto skewers and serve immediately.

Serves 6

GINGER-GARLIC TURKEY BROCHETTES

The relatively bland flavor of turkey takes well to this delicious marinade. Serve the turkey with steamed rice and a steamed green vegetable.

*1 boneless, skinless turkey breast half, about 3 to 3½
  pounds*

GINGER-GARLIC MARINADE
¾ cup dry white wine
¼ cup vegetable oil
3 garlic cloves, pressed
½ cup grated unpeeled fresh ginger

12 bamboo skewers, soaked in water
Chopped fresh parsley or cilantro, for garnish (optional)

1. Dice the turkey into 1¼-inch cubes.

2. In a nonreactive container, combine the wine, oil, and garlic. Gather the grated ginger in your hands and squeeze tightly over the container, allowing the juice to run into the marinade. Discard the grated ginger. Mix the ingredients well. Add the cubed turkey, cover the container, and refrigerate for 2 to 3 hours.

3. Preheat the grill for 10 to 15 minutes, with all the burners on high.

4. While the grill is preheating, pour off the marinade from the container and discard it. Thread the turkey onto the skewers, with the sides of the cubes touching.

5. Once the grill is hot, turn all the burners to medium. Grill the skewered turkey for 15 to 18 minutes, turning the brochettes once or twice.

6. Transfer the turkey to a warm serving platter, garnish with parsley or cilantro if desired, and serve.

Serves 6

⁺⁺◆⁺⁺
TURKEY BURGERS
⁺⁺◆⁺⁺

Not long ago, if you asked your butcher for ground turkey meat, you would have gotten a puzzled look in response. These days, ground turkey meat is readily available in most supermarkets, making short work of this recipe. For the record, my tasters—young and old alike—chose turkey burgers as one of their favorite recipes in this book. Just be sure to toast the hamburger buns, and add a slice of jellied cranberry sauce on top of each turkey burger. Good eating!

1 pound ground turkey
4 tablespoons heavy cream
1 teaspoon salt
1 teaspoon ground white pepper
1 teaspoon seasoned salt
4 tablespoons butter, melted and cooled slightly
4 hamburger buns

1. Preheat the grill for 10 to 15 minutes, with all the burners on high.

2. While the grill is preheating, mix the ground turkey, cream, salt, pepper, and seasoned salt in a bowl. Put a little melted butter on your hands, because the ground turkey is very sticky, and shape the mixture into 4 patties, each about ½ inch thick. Place the patties on a ceramic plate and brush each one on both sides with some of the melted butter. If necessary, refrigerate the patties for up to 4 hours before cooking them.

3. Once the grill is hot, turn all the burners to medium-high. Grill the turkey patties for about 15 to 18 minutes, turning them once.

4. A few minutes before the patties are done, brush the buns with the remaining melted butter and toast them on the grill.

5. Serve the patties in the toasted buns.

Serves 4

•❖•

HERBED CORNISH GAME HENS

•❖•

These Cornish game hens are great hot off the grill, but they're even better served cold or at room temperature as picnic fare.

4 Cornish game hens, each about 1 to 1½ pounds

MARINADE
¾ cup extra-virgin olive oil
¼ cup dry white wine
2 tablespoons Dijon mustard
1½ teaspoons dried rosemary
2 teaspoons dried thyme leaves, crumbled
3 or 4 garlic cloves, pressed
¼ teaspoon fresh-ground black pepper

1. Wash the Cornish game hens inside and out with cold water and pat them dry.

2. Combine all the marinade ingredients in a nonreactive container and mix well. Place the hens in the marinade, cover the container, and refrigerate for 2 to 3 hours, or overnight if desired.

3. Preheat the grill for 10 to 15 minutes, with all the burners on high.

4. While the grill is preheating, drain the marinade from its container into a nonreactive saucepan. Bring the liquid to a boil for a minute or two, remove the pan from the heat, and reserve for basting.

5. Once the grill is hot, turn one burner off and the other(s) to medium. Place the hens, breast side up, over the burner that is off. Close the grill's lid and cook the birds for 1 hour, turning them every 15 or 20 minutes and basting with the boiled marinade.

6. Serve the game hens hot off the grill or at room temperature.

Serves 4 generously

⋄◆⋄

CHINESE CORNISH GAME HENS

⋄◆⋄

Cornish game hens lend themselves well to a Chinese-style marinade. This dish is excellent served with steamed rice and stir-fried vegetables, such as asparagus or broccoli and garlic.

4 Cornish game hens, each about 1 to 1½ pounds

MARINADE
½ cup soy sauce
½ cup sherry
3 tablespoons sesame oil
3 tablespoons brown sugar
½ cup minced green onion
3 garlic cloves, pressed
2 tablespoons grated fresh ginger
⅛ teaspoon cayenne

1. Wash the Cornish game hens inside and out with cold water and pat them dry.

For a terrific picnic dinner, serve Cornish game hens cold the day after they are grilled.

2. Combine all the marinade ingredients in a nonreactive container and mix well. Place the hens in the marinade, cover the container, and refrigerate for 2 to 3 hours, or overnight if desired.

3. Preheat the grill for 10 to 15 minutes, with all the burners on high.

4. While the grill is preheating, drain the marinade from its container into a nonreactive saucepan. Bring the liquid to a boil for a minute or two, remove the pan from the heat, and reserve for basting.

5. Once the grill is hot, turn one burner off and turn the other(s) to medium. Place the game hens over the burner that is off. Close the grill's lid and cook the hens for 60 minutes, turning them every 15 or 20 minutes and basting with the boiled marinade. Serve hot off the grill or at room temperature.

Serves 4 generously

◆

GRILLED QUAIL WITH PANCETTA

◆

Fresh quail are becoming available in more supermarkets across the country. If you like the taste of grilled poultry, you'll probably enjoy quail, especially as it is done here: wrapped in pancetta to add a little extra flavor and moisture.

8 to 12 quail
Olive oil
Lemon juice
Dried thyme leaves, crumbled
Salt and fresh-ground black pepper
8 to 12 thin slices of pancetta (1 slice per quail)

1. Preheat the grill for 10 to 15 minutes, with all the burners on high.

2. While the grill is preheating, flatten the quail according to the directions on page 59, or ask your butcher to do it for you in advance. Rinse the quail well in cold water and pat them dry. Rub each quail with a little olive oil and fresh lemon juice, and then sprinkle each one with thyme, salt, and pepper. Wrap each quail with a slice of pancetta.

3. Once the grill is hot, turn one burner off and turn the other(s) to medium. Position the quail, breast side up, over the burner that is off. Close the grill's lid and cook the birds for about 6 minutes per side, turning them once.

4. Serve hot off the grill or at room temperature.

Serves 4

⋅⋅◆⋅⋅
GRILLED PHEASANT
⋅⋅◆⋅⋅

Farm-raised pheasant is becoming more widely available all the time. It is an elegant and delicious bird, needing only salt and pepper to allow its unique flavor to show through. Serve this dish with Buttered Grilled Carrots (page 173) and Wild Rice Casserole (page 232).

> *1 pheasant, about 2 to 3 pounds*
> *Vegetable oil*
> *Salt and fresh-ground black pepper*

1. Flatten the pheasant according to the directions on page 59, or ask your butcher to do it for you. Rinse the pheasant with cold water and pat it dry. Rub vegetable oil liberally all over the bird, and season with salt and pepper.

2. Preheat the grill for 10 to 15 minutes, with all the burners on high.

3. Once the grill is hot, turn one burner off and turn the other(s) to medium. Place the pheasant, breast up, over the burner that is off. Close the grill's lid and cook the bird for 1 to 1½ hours, turning the pheasant every 15 minutes.

4. Transfer the bird to a carving board. Cover it loosely with a foil tent and let it rest for 10 minutes.

5. Carve the bird as you would a duck, and serve warm.

Serves 4

CHAPTER FOUR

◆

BEEF

◆

CHAPTER FOUR
BEEF

◆

Over the past few years, most Americans have reduced the amount of beef they eat on a regular basis. If you follow this generally healthful trend, when you do eat beef, treat yourself to the very best you can find. The best beef will be labeled "prime," the meat will be deep red, and the fat will be creamy white. The best beef also should have marbling—thin streaks of creamy yellow fat running through the meat—which adds immeasurably to its flavor and succulence. "Choice" beef is next in quality and is usually fine for most grilling. "Select" is the least expensive grade.

Many cuts of beef benefit from the tenderizing effects of marinating. Whether or not the meat is marinated, remove it from the refrigerator about 30 minutes before you are ready to grill, to bring the temperature of the meat closer to room temperature.

JUDGING DONENESS
..◆..

Remember that beef continues to cook after it is taken off the grill. You should remove beef from the grill, especially large cuts such as roasts, when its internal temperature registers about 5 to 10 degrees shy of the desired temperature. Place the meat on a carving board, cover it loosely with a foil tent, and let it rest for 10 to 15 minutes before carving. The resting period not only allows the meat to reach the level of doneness you desire, but also allows flavorful juices to be reabsorbed into the meat, creating a more succulent dish.

Beef is considered rare at 140° F, medium at 160° F, and well-done at 170° F.

⋄◆⋄
FILET MIGNON WITH MARINATED GRILLED MUSHROOMS
⋄◆⋄

If you find that you're eating less red meat these days, you may also find that when you have a craving for it, you want a really good steak. This is it. The classic pairing of filet mignon and mushrooms is even better when both are cooked on the grill. Excellent side dishes include Rosemary Potato Wedges (page 192) and Garlicky Grilled Tomatoes (page 196).

MARINATED MUSHROOMS
½ cup dry red wine
¼ cup extra-virgin olive oil
Juice of ½ lemon
1 large garlic clove, pressed
2 teaspoons crumbled whole fresh thyme leaves
1 teaspoon salt
½ teaspoon fresh-cracked peppercorns
1 pound whole mushrooms, washed and stems trimmed

TO MARINATE OR NOT TO MARINATE?
◆

Beef steaks fall into two categories: those that benefit from marinating and those that do not. Tougher cuts should be marinated for 2 to 4 hours in the refrigerator. Twenty to 30 minutes before grilling, remove the meat from the refrigerator, to allow the meat to come to near room temperature.

Steaks That Need Marinating
Chuck
Eye of the round
Flank
Round
Sirloin
Skirt
Top round

Steaks That Need No Marinating
Club
Filet mignon
Kansas City
Loin
New York
Porterhouse
Rib
Shell
Sirloin (may also be marinated)
Strip
T-bone
Tenderloin

A good sauce for leftover cold sliced steak? Equal parts sour cream, mayonnaise, and grated horserad-ish, with a little Dijon mustard.

6 bamboo skewers, soaked in water

4 filet mignon steaks, each about 1 to 1½ inches thick
Olive oil
Fresh-cracked peppercorns

1. To make the marinated mushrooms, combine all the in-gredients except the mushrooms in a nonreactive bowl and mix well. Toss the mushrooms in the marinade, cover the bowl, and re-frigerate for 1 to 2 hours, stirring the mushrooms occasionally.

2. Brush the steaks with olive oil and sprinkle liberally with the cracked peppercorns.

3. Preheat the grill for 10 to 15 minutes, with all the burners on high.

4. While the grill is preheating, drain the marinade from the bowl and discard it. Thread the mushrooms onto the skewers for easier handling.

5. Once the grill is hot, place the steaks directly over the burners, which are still on high, and close the grill's lid. Sear only one side of the steaks, leaving them over the heat for about 2 minutes for 1-inch steaks, 4 minutes for 1½-inch steaks. After searing the steaks on one side, turn one burner off and turn the other(s) to medium. Flip the steaks (so the seared side is up), move them directly over the burner that is now off, and place the skewered mushrooms next to them. Close the grill's lid and finish cooking the steaks, turning them once. After searing, 1-inch steaks will take 4 to 5 minutes to cook to rare, 5 to 7 minutes to cook to medium, and 7 to 9 minutes to cook to well-done. Allow slightly more time for 1½-inch steaks. Depending on their size, the mushrooms will be cooked tender in about 8 to 12 minutes, so you may have to continue cooking them after the steaks are done.

6. Serve the steaks hot off the grill, sur-rounded by the mushrooms.

Serves 4

⋄◆⋄

CHÂTEAUBRIAND WITH GREEN PEPPERCORN SAUCE

⋄◆⋄

This recipe is a variation on the famous French steak *au poivre verte*. It's an impressive dish with assertive flavors, best served with simple side dishes, such as baked potatoes and steamed broccoli or asparagus. If you're planning to serve a red wine, choose something "big," because this meal will stand up to the biggest red wine in town.

Note: The name *Châteaubriand* is something of a misnomer. Originally it referred to the very best filet steak, cut unusually thick—at least 2 inches. Nowadays, the term *Châteaubriand* may refer to a variety of cuts of beef (most often the sirloin), the common denominator being the thickness of the cut.

3-pound to 4-pound Châteaubriand, about 2 inches thick
3 or 4 garlic cloves, peeled and cut into about a dozen
    slivers total
Olive oil
Fresh-ground black pepper

GREEN PEPPERCORN SAUCE
2 tablespoons butter
3 tablespoons chopped shallots or green onions (white
    part only)
1 cup beef stock
½ cup dry red wine
2 to 3 tablespoons green peppercorns (preferably brine-
    packed)
1 tablespoon Dijon mustard

1. Using the tip of a sharp knife, make about 6 incisions on each side of the steak, deep enough to hold a sliver of garlic. Insert a sliver of garlic into each incision. Brush the steaks with olive oil and dust them liberally with fresh-ground black pepper.

2. Preheat the grill for 10 to 15 minutes, with all the burners on high.

3. While the grill is preheating, make the sauce. In a small saucepan over medium heat, melt the butter. Add the shallots or green onions and sauté until soft and transparent, about 3 minutes. Add the stock, wine, and green peppercorns, and cook the sauce over medium-high heat for 5 to 7 minutes, stirring occasionally. Whisk in the Dijon mustard, remove the pan from the heat, and reserve until serving time.

4. Once the grill is hot, place the steak directly over the burners, which are still on high, and close the grill's lid. Sear only one side of the steak, for about 4 minutes. After searing the steak on one side, turn one burner off and turn the other(s) to medium. Flip the steak (so the seared side is up), and move it directly over the burner that is now off. Close the grill's lid and finish cooking the steak, turning it once. After searing, 2-inch Châteaubriand will take about 10 to 13 minutes to reach the rare stage (140° F), 13 to 15 minutes to reach medium (160° F), and 15 to 19 minutes to reach well-done (170° F).

5. Transfer the steak to a carving board, cover it loosely with a foil tent, and let it rest for 10 to 15 minutes. Meanwhile, reheat the sauce.

6. To serve, slice the meat thick or thin, as desired. Pour a couple of tablespoons of sauce over each portion, and serve.

Serves 6 to 8

> *Count on each person eating about one-third to one-half pound of beef, not including bones.*

STEAKS WITH ROQUEFORT BUTTER

This timeless combination—a great steak, hot off the grill, with a dollop of Roquefort butter melting on top—is as good today as it ever was. If real French Roquefort cheese is not available, substitute a domestic blue cheese.

4 steaks (filet mignon, strip, rib-eye, or another favorite)
Olive oil
Fresh-ground black pepper

ROQUEFORT BUTTER
6 tablespoons butter, at room temperature
2 ounces Roquefort cheese
1 garlic clove, pressed

1. Brush the steaks with olive oil and dust them liberally with pepper.

2. Preheat the grill for 10 to 15 minutes, with all the burners on high.

3. While the grill is preheating, make the Roquefort butter. In a small bowl, combine the butter, Roquefort cheese, and garlic. Mix thoroughly with a fork and reserve until serving time.

4. Once the grill is hot, place the steaks directly over the burners, which are still on high, and close the grill's lid. Sear only one side of the steaks, about 2 minutes for 1-inch steaks, 4 minutes for 1½-inch steaks. After searing the steaks on one side, turn one burner off and turn the other(s) to medium. Flip the steaks (so the seared side is up), and move them directly over the burner that is now off. Close the grill's lid and finish cooking the steaks, turning them once. After searing, 1-inch steaks will take 4 to 5 minutes to cook to rare, 5 to 7 minutes to cook to medium, and 7 to 9 minutes to cook to well-done. Allow slightly more time for 1½-inch steaks.

5. Serve hot off the grill with a tablespoon or so of the Roquefort butter on top.

Serves 4

STRIP STEAKS WITH GRILLED POTATO SKINS

Whether you call them New York strip steaks or Kansas City strip steaks, almost every beef lover calls them good. In Pasadena, California, there was a legendary steak house called Monty's that not only served a great strip steak, but also may have invented the grilled potato skin. To many potato lovers, the skin is the best part, made even better by grilling.

4 large Idaho or russet baking potatoes
4 strip steaks, each about 1 to 1½ inches thick
Olive oil
Fresh-ground black pepper
Butter, sour cream, chopped chives, and salt and pepper,
*   for topping (optional)*

1. Scrub the potatoes well under cold water. Using the tip of a sharp knife, poke a few steam vents in each potato. Bake the potatoes in a preheated 350° F oven for 60 minutes. Remove the potatoes from the oven and let them cool.

2. Brush the steaks with olive oil and dust them liberally with pepper.

3. Preheat the grill for 10 to 15 minutes, with all the burners on high.

4. While the grill is preheating, cut a slit lengthwise in each baked potato and remove all but ¼ inch or so of the flesh. Flatten each potato with the heel of your hand.

5. Once the grill is hot, place the steaks directly over the burners, which are still on high, and close the grill's lid. Sear only one side of the steaks, about 2 minutes for 1-inch steaks, 4 minutes for 1½-inch steaks. After searing the steaks on one side, turn one burner off and turn the other(s) to medium. Flip the steaks (so the seared side is up), move them directly over the burner that is now off, and place the potato skins next to them. Close the grill's lid and finish cooking the steaks, turning the meat and the potatoes once, at the same time. After searing, 1-inch steaks will take 4 to 5 minutes to cook to rare, 5 to 7 minutes to cook to medium, and 7 to 9 minutes to cook to well-done. You can remove the potato skins from the grill when you remove the steaks.

6. Serve the steaks hot off the grill with the potato skins on the side. Top the skins with plenty of butter, sour cream, chives, and salt and pepper, if you wish.

Serves 4

RIB-EYE STEAKS WITH CHILI BUTTER

Real steak lovers swear by the rib-eye steak for taste and texture. Though not the most refined of cuts, it's what many people want when they're hungry for a big steak with lots of big steak flavor.

CHILI BUTTER
½ cup salted butter, at room temperature
1 tablespoon chili powder
1 large garlic clove, pressed
Juice of 1 lime

4 rib-eye steaks, each about 1 to 1½ inches thick
Olive oil
Fresh-ground black pepper

The very best beef—labeled "prime"—is deep red, has creamy-white fat, and is streaked through with thin bands of fat, known as marbling.

1. To make the chili butter, combine all of the ingredients in a bowl and whip with a fork until they are well blended. Cover the bowl and refrigerate until needed.

2. Brush the steaks with olive oil and dust them liberally with pepper.

3. Preheat the grill for 10 to 15 minutes, with all the burners on high.

4. Once the grill is hot, place the steaks directly over the burners, which are still on high, and close the grill's lid. Sear only one side of the steaks, about 2 minutes for 1-inch steaks, 4 minutes for 1½-inch steaks. After searing the steaks on one side, turn one burner off and turn the other(s) to medium. Flip the steaks (so the seared side is up), and move them directly over the burner that is now off. Close the grill's lid and finish cooking the steaks, turning them once. After searing, 1-inch steaks will take 4 to 5 minutes to cook to rare, 5 to 7 minutes to cook to medium, and 7 to 9 minutes to cook to well-done. Allow slightly more time for 1½-inch steaks.

5. Serve the steaks hot off the grill, with a couple of tablespoons of the chili butter on top of each one.

Serves 4

T-BONE PICANTE

The dry rub in this recipe transforms an ordinary T-bone into a spicy steak with a Southwestern accent. Team it up with Cowpoke Beans (page 224) and steamed rice for a hearty, mouthwatering meal.

DRY RUB

4 tablespoons paprika
2 tablespoons chili powder
2 tablespoons ground cumin
1 tablespoon ground oregano
1 tablespoon ground black pepper
1 tablespoon ground white pepper
*2 teaspoons cayenne (optional: omit if you don't want the
    meat spicy-hot)*
2 tablespoons dark brown sugar
2 tablespoons salt
1 tablespoon sugar

4 T-bone steaks, each about 1 to 1½ inches thick

1. Combine all the dry rub ingredients in a bowl and mix well.
Evenly dust the steaks with the mixture and rub it in with your
fingers. Cover the steaks and refrigerate for 1 to 2 hours. Store leftover dry rub in a lidded jar in the freezer.

2. Preheat the grill for 10 to 15 minutes, with all the burners
on high.

3. Once the grill is hot, place the steaks directly over the
burners, which are still on high, and close the grill's lid. Sear only one
side of the steaks, about 2 minutes for 1-inch steaks, 4 minutes for
1½-inch steaks. After searing the steaks on one side, turn one burner
off and turn the other(s) to medium. Flip the steaks (so the seared
side is up), and move them directly over the burner that is now off.
Close the grill's lid and finish cooking the steaks, turning them once.
After searing, 1-inch steaks will take 4 to 5 minutes to cook to rare,
5 to 7 minutes to cook to medium, and 7 to 9 minutes to cook to
well-done. Allow slightly more time for 1½-inch steaks.

4. Serve hot off the grill.

Serves 4

GARLIC-STUDDED LONDON BROIL

Serve this steak hot off the grill, or cold the next day for out-of-this-world steak sandwiches.

3-pound to 4-pound London broil, about 2 inches thick
3 or 4 garlic cloves, peeled and cut into about a dozen
*   slivers total*
Olive oil
Fresh-ground black pepper

1. Using the tip of a sharp knife, make about 6 incisions on each side of the steak, deep enough to hold a sliver of garlic. Insert a sliver of garlic into each incision. Brush the meat with olive oil and dust it liberally with pepper.

2. Preheat the grill for 10 to 15 minutes, with all the burners on high.

3. Once the grill is hot, place the steak directly over the burners, which are still on high, and close the grill's lid. Sear only one side of the steak, for about 4 minutes. After searing the steak on one side, turn one burner off and turn the other(s) to medium. Flip the steak (so the seared side is up), and move it directly over the burner that is now off. Close the grill's lid and finish cooking the steak, turning it once. After searing, 2-inch London broil will take about 10 to 13 minutes to reach the rare stage (140° F), 13 to 15 minutes to reach medium (160° F), and 15 to 19 minutes to reach well-done (170° F).

4. Transfer the meat to a carving board, cover it loosely with a foil tent, and let it rest for 10 to 15 minutes.

5. Slice the steak thick or thin, as desired, and serve.

Serves 6 to 8

LONDON BROIL WITH BLACK BEAN AND CORN SALSA

BLACK BEAN AND CORN SALSA
¾ cup canned black beans, rinsed and drained
¾ cup frozen whole kernel corn, thawed
¼ cup minced onion
¼ cup diced green bell pepper
2 tablespoons vegetable oil
1 tablespoon fresh lime juice
3 tablespoons minced fresh cilantro
¼ teaspoon salt
Fresh-ground black pepper to taste

3-pound to 4-pound London broil, about 2 inches thick
Olive oil
Fresh-ground black pepper

1. Combine all the salsa ingredients in a bowl and mix well. Refrigerate the salsa until serving time.

2. Brush the steak with olive oil and dust it liberally with black pepper.

3. Preheat the grill for 10 to 15 minutes, with all the burners on high.

4. Once the grill is hot, place the steak directly over the burners, which are still on high, and close the grill's lid. Sear only one side of the steak, for about 4 minutes. After searing the steak on one side, turn one burner off and turn the other(s) to medium. Flip the steak (so the seared side is up), and move it directly over the burner that is now off. Close the grill's lid and finish cooking the steak, turning it once. After searing, 2-inch London broil will take about 10 to 13 minutes to reach the rare stage (140° F), 13 to 15 minutes to reach medium (160° F), and 15 to 19 minutes to reach well-done (170° F).

5. Transfer the meat to a carving board, cover it loosely with a foil tent, and let it rest for 10 to 15 minutes.

6. Slice the meat thin, top each portion with some black bean and corn salsa, and serve.

Serves 6 to 8

EVERYBODY'S FAVORITE FLANK STEAK

Flank steaks, though they can be tough if they aren't marinated before grilling, are one of the tastiest (and leanest) cuts of beef. Given their large surface area, they take well to marinades, and they cook up in a hurry, too. Serve thin-sliced flank steak with Rosemary Potato Wedges (page 192), or make it into delicious steak sandwiches.

MARINADE
¼ cup vegetable or olive oil
¼ cup soy sauce
½ cup dry sherry
2 garlic cloves, pressed
1 small onion, minced
1½ teaspoons ground dried ginger
1 to 2 teaspoons fresh-ground black pepper

1 flank steak, about 2 to 3 pounds

1. In a nonreactive container, mix together all the marinade ingredients. Place the flank steak in the marinade, turning the meat several times to coat it on both sides. Cover the container and refrigerate for at least 1 hour, turning the steak once or twice in the marinade.

2. Preheat the grill for 10 to 15 minutes with all the burners on high.

3. Once the grill is hot, turn one burner off and turn the other(s) to medium. Drain the marinade from its container and discard it. Sear the flank steak quickly on both sides (about 1 to 2 minutes per side) over one of the burners that is on. After searing the steak, move it directly over the burner that is off, close the grill's lid, and cook the steak for another 18 to 20 minutes, turning it once. The flank steak will be cooked medium; adjust the cooking time slightly for rare or well-done steak.

4. Transfer the steak to a cutting board, cover it loosely with a foil tent, and let it rest for 5 minutes.

As long as you're cooking one flank steak, you might as well cook two: leftovers make a first-rate sliced steak sandwich the following day.

5. Using a sharp carving knife held at a 45-degree angle, cut the flank steak into thin slices. Serve hot off the grill with juices that accumulated on the cutting board, or at room temperature.

Serves 4 to 6

SPICY FLANK STEAK

MARINADE
4-inch chunk unpeeled fresh ginger, grated
¼ cup soy sauce
¼ cup water
2 tablespoons vegetable oil
2 tablespoons rice wine vinegar
2 to 3 large garlic cloves, pressed
½ teaspoon cayenne

1 flank steak, about 2 to 3 pounds
Chopped fresh mint and cilantro, for garnish (optional)

1. To make the marinade, gather up the grated ginger in your hands and squeeze the juice into a nonreactive container. Add the remaining marinade ingredients and mix well. Place the flank steak in the marinade, turning the steak several times to coat it well, cover the container, and refrigerate for 2 to 3 hours. Turn the flank steak a few times while it marinates.

2. Preheat the grill for 10 to 15 minutes, with all the burners on high.

3. Once the grill is hot, turn one burner off and turn the other(s) to medium. Drain the marinade from its container and discard it. Sear the flank steak quickly on both sides (about 1 to 2 minutes per side) over one of the burners that is on. After searing the steak, move it directly over the burner that is off, close the grill's lid, and cook the steak for another 18 to 20 minutes, turning it once. The flank steak will be cooked medium; adjust the cooking time slightly for rare or well-done steak.

4. Transfer the steak to a carving board, cover it loosely with a foil tent, and let it rest for 5 minutes.

Always carve flank steak across the grain. For the most attractive slices, hold your knife at a 45-degree angle as you slice the meat.

5. Using a sharp carving knife held at a 45-degree angle, cut the flank steak into thin slices. Garnish with mint and cilantro, if desired, and serve.

Serves 4 to 6

••◆••

TRIED-AND-TRUE MARINATED BEEF KEBOBS

••◆••

Most beef cut for kebobs tends to be a little on the tough side; the marinade in this recipe will not only tenderize the meat, but also give it a flavor that everyone seems to love.

MARINADE
½ cup dry sherry
¼ cup soy sauce
3 tablespoons vegetable oil
2 garlic cloves, pressed
1 small onion, minced
1½ teaspoons ground dried ginger

2 pounds round, flank, or chuck steak, cut in 1-inch
   cubes
12 bamboo skewers, soaked in water

1. Combine all the marinade ingredients in a nonreactive container and mix well. Add the beef cubes to the marinade, making sure they are all submerged. Cover the container and refrigerate for 2 to 3 hours, or overnight if desired.

2. Preheat the grill for 10 to 15 minutes, with all the burners on high.

3. While the grill is preheating, drain the marinade from the container and discard it. Thread the marinated beef onto the skewers, with the sides of the pieces touching.

4. Once the grill is hot, turn all the burners to medium. Place the skewers on the grill and cook the meat for about 8 to 12 minutes, turning the skewers once or twice.

5. Serve the skewered beef hot off the grill.

Serves 4 generously

◆

FLANK STEAK SANDWICHES WITH GRILLED BELL PEPPERS AND ONIONS

◆

Thin slices of flank steak and a mound of grilled peppers and onions make a delicious sandwich—a classic combination that's hard to put down.

MARINADE
¼ cup vegetable or olive oil
¼ cup soy sauce
½ cup dry sherry
1 to 2 teaspoons fresh-ground black pepper

1 flank steak, about 2 to 3 pounds
2 whole medium onions
2 whole green bell peppers
Vegetable oil
Salt and fresh-ground black pepper
Sliced bread or buns, warmed

1. In a nonreactive container, mix together all the marinade ingredients. Place the flank steak in the marinade, turning the steak several times to coat it well, cover the container, and refrigerate for at least 1 hour. Turn the flank steak once or twice while it marinates.

2. Preheat the grill for 10 to 15 minutes, with all the burners on high.

3. While the grill is preheating, peel the onions, cut them into ⅜-inch-thick slices, and coat them with oil. Wash and dry the bell peppers and then coat them with oil.

4. Once the grill is hot, turn one burner off and turn the other(s) to medium. Drain the marinade from the container and discard it. Sear the flank steak quickly on both sides (about 1 to 2 minutes per side) directly over one of the burners that is on. After searing the meat, move it directly over the burner that is off. Surround the meat with the onion slices and bell peppers. Close the grill's lid. Turn the meat once during the cooking, and turn the vegetables at the same time. The onion slices will be done when they are soft and slightly brown, in about 6 to 8 minutes; the peppers will be done when they have collapsed on themselves, in 10 to 20 minutes. The meat should cook for a total of 18 to 20 minutes for a medium steak. Adjust the cooking time slightly for rare or well-done meat, as you wish.

5. Transfer the steak to a cutting board, cover it loosely with a foil tent, and let it rest for 5 minutes.

6. While the steak is resting, remove the stems and seeds from the grilled peppers, and slice the peppers ⅜ inch thick. Combine the pepper and onion slices in a bowl and toss with a little salt and pepper.

7. Using a sharp carving knife held at a 45-degree angle, cut the flank steak into thin slices. Serve the slices of steak, topped with the pepper-and-onion mixture, on warm sliced bread or buns.

Serves 4 generously

•◆•

INDONESIAN-STYLE BEEF SATÉ

•◆•

Spicy foods are refreshing when the temperature is rising through the roof. The following recipe is a somewhat improbable combination of several Indonesian cuisines. This dish is excellent with ice-cold beer.

2-pound to 3-pound London broil, 1 to 1½ inches thick

PEANUT SAUCE
½ cup peanut butter (chunky or smooth)
1 cup chicken or vegetable stock
2 tablespoons soy sauce
1 tablespoon brown sugar
1 to 2 teaspoons Tabasco sauce

MARINADE
½ cup sake

¼ cup soy sauce
3 tablespoons vegetable oil
4 tablespoons grated fresh ginger
4 tablespoons chopped green onions
1 or 2 fresh chile peppers, minced (or 1 to 2 teaspoons
    dried red pepper flakes)

12 bamboo skewers, soaked in water

Whole lettuce leaves
Cooked Asian rice noodles, chilled, or steamed white rice
Chopped fresh cilantro and mint

1. To make slicing the steak much easier, put it in the freezer for 30 to 45 minutes, until it starts to get firm.

2. In a medium saucepan, combine all the peanut sauce ingredients. Whisk the sauce over medium-high heat until it thickens. Remove the pan from the heat and reserve the sauce until serving time.

3. Combine all the marinade ingredients in a nonreactive container and mix well. Cut the steak into 1/4-inch slices, add the meat to the marinade, cover the container, and refrigerate for 15 to 30 minutes.

4. Preheat the grill for 10 to 15 minutes, with all the burners on high.

5. While the grill is preheating, drain the marinade from the container and discard it. Thread or weave the marinated beef onto the skewers, keeping the meat as flat as possible.

6. Once the grill is hot, turn all the burners to medium. Place the skewers directly over the heat and grill for 8 to 12 minutes, turning them once.

7. Meanwhile, reheat the peanut sauce and then transfer it to a serving bowl. Arrange the lettuce leaves on a large platter. Place the rice or noodles in one serving bowl, the cilantro in another, and the mint in another.

8. Serve the meat and accompaniments family style. Each person takes one lettuce leaf, fills it partially with noodles or steamed rice, a couple of slices of grilled beef, some peanut sauce, and the

chopped cilantro and mint, and then folds the leaf around the filling like a tortilla.

Serves 6 to 8

⁖◆⁖

SKEWERED BEEF BOURGUIGNON

⁖◆⁖

This recipe may sound like one of those well-intentioned
but nevertheless ill-advised concoctions from a home arts
magazine, circa 1962, but rest assured that it is as tasty as it is
up-to-date.

MARINADE
2 cups dry red wine
¼ cup extra-virgin olive oil
2 bay leaves
½ teaspoon dried thyme leaves
½ teaspoon dried rosemary
1 teaspoon salt
½ teaspoon fresh-ground black pepper

3 pounds boneless beef, cut into 2-inch chunks
16 small to medium mushrooms, washed and stems
  trimmed
16 small white boiling onions, parboiled and skinned
4 bacon strips, partially cooked, cut into 4 pieces per slice
2 dozen bamboo skewers, soaked in water

Buttered, parslied noodles

1. Combine all the marinade ingredients in a nonreactive container and mix well. Add the beef cubes and the mushrooms, cover the container, and refrigerate for 4 to 6 hours.

2. Preheat the grill for 10 to 15 minutes, with all the burners
on high.

3. While the grill is preheating, drain the marinade from the
container and discard it. Thread the beef, mushrooms, onions, and
bacon onto the skewers, alternating each as you go.

4. Once the grill is hot, turn all the burners to medium. Place the kebobs on the grill and cook for about 8 to 12 minutes, turning the food once or twice.

5. Transfer the kebobs to your work surface, remove the skewers, and serve on top of the noodles.

Serves 6 to 8

TERIYAKI BEEF WITH GREEN ONIONS AND MUSHROOMS

2-pound to 3-pound London broil, 1 to 1½ inches thick
3 bunches green onions, white part cut into 1¼-inch
   pieces
1 pound white mushrooms, washed and stems trimmed
12-ounce bottle teriyaki sauce

12 bamboo skewers, soaked in water

1. To make slicing the steak much easier, put it in the freezer for 30 to 45 minutes, until it starts to get firm.

2. Cut the steak into ¼-inch-thick slices.

3. About 30 minutes before grilling, combine the beef, green onions, and mushrooms with the teriyaki sauce in a bowl. Toss the beef and vegetables to coat them well.

4. Preheat the grill for 10 to 15 minutes, with all the burners on high.

5. While the grill is preheating, thread the marinated beef onto the skewers, alternating with pieces of green onion and mushrooms. The strips of meat should weave among the vegetables.

6. Once the grill is hot, turn all the burners to medium. Grill the skewers for 8 to 12 minutes, turning them once.

7. Serve hot off the grill.

Serves 6 to 8

THE CLASSIC BURGER

This all-American original too often turns out disappointing when cooked at home. The problem, in most cases, is making the hamburger too thick, or using meat that's too lean. If you're really watching your fat intake, by all means use lean ground beef; otherwise, use ground chuck (which yields a much juicier burger) and don't make the patties any thicker than ¾ inch. For a truly delicious burger, grill ¼-inch slices of onion, ½-inch slices of tomato, and buttered hamburger buns while you're grilling the burgers. Outstanding!

1 pound ground chuck (or lean ground beef, if desired)
½ teaspoon salt
½ teaspoon fresh-ground black pepper

1. Preheat the grill for 10 to 15 minutes, with all the burners on high.

2. While the grill is preheating, mix the ground beef, salt, and pepper and shape the beef into 4 patties, each about ½ to ¾ inch thick.

3. Once the grill is hot, turn all the burners to medium. Grill the burgers for about 4 to 5 minutes per side for medium, about 6 minutes per side for well-done, turning them once.

4. Serve hot off the grill.

Serves 4

> *Resist the temptation to press down with your spatula on hamburger patties as they're grilling: it does nothing but squeeze flavorful juices out of the meat.*

WHOLE TENDERLOIN OF BEEF WITH BÉARNAISE SAUCE

A tenderloin roast beef falls into the category of "company food," especially when paired with the classic béarnaise sauce. In truth, few things are as easy to cook as a tenderloin roast. However, to cook any roast to perfection, use a meat thermometer: you can't accurately judge doneness by eye alone. Remember to take the roast off the grill when it is about 10 degrees shy of the desired temperature; the roast will continue to cook as it rests on the carving board. Tenderloin roasts come in half and whole sizes; half usually runs 2 to 3 pounds, and whole runs 4 to 5 pounds. Count on ⅓ to ½ pound per person.

Béarnaise sauce, tarragon-flavored emulsified butter sauce, goes exceptionally well with both beef and lamb. Some people follow the time-honored method of making béarnaise in a double-boiler, but I suggest that you use an electric blender, which is much faster and easier.

1 tenderloin roast beef, about 4 to 5 pounds
Olive oil
Fresh-cracked peppercorns

BÉARNAISE SAUCE
1 tablespoon minced shallot or onion
3 tablespoons white wine vinegar
1 teaspoon coarse-ground black pepper
1 teaspoon dried tarragon, or 2 to 3 sprigs fresh tarragon,
  minced
3 egg yolks, at room temperature
1 cup butter, melted and still hot

1. Rub the tenderloin with olive oil and sprinkle it liberally with cracked pepper.

2. Preheat the grill for 10 to 15 minutes, with all the burners on high.

3. Once the grill is hot, turn one burner off and turn the other(s) to medium. Place the roast, fat side up, over the burner that is off. Close the grill's lid and cook the tenderloin until a meat thermometer registers about 5 to 10 degrees shy of the desired temperature (140° F for rare, 160° F for medium, 170° F for well-done). A 4-to-5-pound tenderloin will take from 50 to 90 minutes to cook to the rare stage.

4. While the tenderloin roasts, prepare the béarnaise sauce. Combine the shallot or onion, white wine vinegar, pepper, and tarragon in a small saucepan and bring to a boil. Boil the mixture rapidly over high heat until only 1 or 2 teaspoons of liquid remain. Watch carefully, swirling the mixture around almost constantly to avoid scorching. Remove the pan from the stove and allow the mixture to cool.

5. Combine the egg yolks and the cooled shallot-and-vinegar mixture in a blender. Process until well blended, about 1 minute or so. Turn the blender to high and add the hot butter, drip by drip at first, gradually increasing it to a steady stream as the mixture begins to thicken. Pour the sauce into a prewarmed thermos bottle. It will keep without curdling or "breaking" for 2 hours or more.

6. When the roast is done, transfer it to a carving board, cover it loosely with a foil tent, and allow it to rest for 10 minutes or so.

7. Carve the meat in thick slices (like individual filet mignon steaks) or thin slices, as desired. Serve with a small amount of the delightfully rich and flavorful béarnaise sauce.

Serves 12 to 15

•✦•

STANDING RIB ROAST WITH HORSERADISH SAUCE

•✦•

A gas grill makes preparation of this "company meal" a snap. Also, grilling outside keeps the kitchen (and the cook) cool, and produces a roast superior to any oven dweller. If you buy your meat from an old-fashioned market, have the butcher cut off the short ribs and the chine bone, loosen the feather bones, and tie the whole roast with string. Prepackaged rib roasts are usually offered this way.

4-pound to 6-pound standing rib roast
Salt and fresh-ground black pepper

HORSERADISH SAUCE
½ cup sour cream
¼ cup pure grated horseradish
¼ cup mayonnaise
1 tablespoon red wine vinegar
½ teaspoon salt
1 teaspoon fresh-ground black pepper

1. Preheat the grill for 10 to 15 minutes, with all the burners on high.

2. While the grill is preheating, dust the roast liberally with salt and pepper. Place the roast on a rack in a roasting pan (a disposable aluminum one is fine).

3. Once the grill is hot, turn one burner off and turn the other(s) to medium. Position the roast over the burner that is off, close the grill's lid, and cook until a meat thermometer registers about 5 to 10 degrees shy of the desired temperature (140° F for rare, 160° F for medium, 170° F for well-done). A 4-to-6-pound standing rib roast will take from 1¼ to 2¼ hours to cook to the rare stage, 2¼ to 2¾ hours for medium, and from 2¾ to 3¼ hours for well-done.

4. While the roast cooks, combine all of the horseradish sauce ingredients in a bowl and mix well. Refrigerate the sauce until serving time.

5. When the roast is done, transfer it to a carving board, cover it loosely with a foil tent, and let it rest for 10 minutes or so.

6. Carve the roast into thick or thin slices, as desired. Serve with the horseradish sauce on the side.

Serves 8 to 10

⁺⁺◆⁺⁺
REAL TASTY BEEF BRISKET
⁺⁺◆⁺⁺

There are few things better than a well-prepared beef brisket—guaranteed to turn any event into a party. But few things are more mysteriously difficult to cook well. With the following procedure, we think we've got you covered, not incidentally because the gas grill seems to be particularly well suited to beef brisket. Because of the long cooking time (6 to 7 hours), this recipe almost demands a stay-at-home cook, or one on a weekend party schedule. Also, be sure you have enough propane to undertake this day-long project.

Note: If you want to serve truly authentic, Kansas City–style brisket, do it this way: Wrap 2 or 3 thin slices of brisket in a single slice of squishy white sandwich bread, add a little coleslaw, a few sour dill pickle chips, and a squeeze or two of your favorite bottled barbecue sauce, and fold it in half.

BASTING SAUCE
4 tablespoons paprika
1 tablespoon ground black pepper
1 tablespoon ground white pepper
2 tablespoons chili powder
2 tablespoons ground cumin
1 tablespoon ground oregano
2 teaspoons cayenne
2 tablespoons salt
2 tablespoons dark brown sugar
1 tablespoon sugar
½ cup cider vinegar
½ cup water
½ cup soy sauce
¼ cup Worcestershire sauce

5-pound to 6-pound beef brisket, fat trimmed to about
   ¼ inch on one side

1. To make the basting sauce, combine the spices, salt, and sugars in a bowl and mix until thoroughly blended. Add the vinegar, water, soy sauce, and Worcestershire to the dry ingredients and mix well. *Note:* If there are people in the crowd who really don't care for heat (as in *picante,* not *caliente*), omit the cayenne altogether. Brush some of the basting sauce onto the brisket.

2. Preheat the grill for 10 to 15 minutes, with all the burners on high.

3. Once the grill is hot, turn one burner off and turn the other(s) to medium. Place the brisket, fat side up, over the burner that is off. Close the grill's lid and cook, without turning the meat, for 6 hours. Baste the brisket with the sauce once or twice an hour.

4. Remove the brisket from the grill and wrap it in aluminum foil. Return the foil-wrapped brisket to the grill, in the same position as before, and cook for 60 minutes longer. The meat should be completely fork-tender.

5. Place the wrapped brisket in the refrigerator for an hour or so.

6. To serve, cut into thin slices.

Serves 8

··◆··
CHUCK WAGON CHUCK ROAST
··◆··

This hearty fare is great for serving a crowd. There's no need to marinate this steak; just baste it frequently during the cooking process. For an unusual but delicious salad course, try combining fresh orange and red onion slices on a bed of lettuce leaves. Dress with a simple oil-and-vinegar mixture and garnish with chopped fresh cilantro, if desired. And remember, we're in chuck wagon mode here, so when it comes to side dishes, think about Cowpoke Beans (page 224), "Baked" Potatoes on the Grill (page 190), or even cornbread.

BASTING SAUCE
½ cup vegetable oil
¾ cup beer
2 tablespoons chili powder
2 teaspoons ground cumin
1 teaspoon dried oregano leaves
1 teaspoon salt
1 teaspoon fresh-ground black pepper

4-pound to 6-pound chuck roast, about 1½ to 2 inches
   thick

1. Preheat the grill for 10 to 15 minutes, with all the burners on high.

2. While the grill is preheating, combine all of the basting sauce ingredients in a bowl and mix well. Coat the roast liberally with the basting sauce.

3. Once the grill is hot, turn one burner off and turn the other(s) to medium. Place the roast over the burner that is off. Close the grill's lid and cook the chuck roast until a meat thermometer registers about 5 to 10 degrees shy of the desired temperature (140° F for rare, 160° F for medium, 170° F for well-done). Brush the roast with the basting sauce every 15 minutes or so. Turn the roast once, halfway through the cooking time. A 4-to-6-pound chuck roast will take 1 to 1¼ hours to cook to the rare stage, 1¼ to 1¾ hours for medium, and 1¾ to 2 hours for well-done.

4. Transfer the roast to a carving board, cover it loosely with a foil tent, and let it rest for 10 minutes or so.

5. To serve, carve the meat on the diagonal into thin slices.

Serves 6 to 8

BONELESS MARINATED CHUCK ROAST

MARINADE
½ cup dry sherry
¼ cup vegetable oil
¼ cup soy sauce
2 garlic cloves, pressed
1 small onion, minced
¼ teaspoon fresh-ground black pepper

4-pound to 6-pound boneless chuck roast

1. Combine all of the marinade ingredients in a nonreactive container and mix well. Add the chuck roast, turn the meat to coat it well, cover the container, and refrigerate for 3 to 4 hours, or overnight if desired. Turn the roast several times while it marinates.

2. Preheat the grill for 10 to 15 minutes, with all the burners on high.

3. Once the grill is hot, turn one burner off and turn the other(s) to medium. Drain the marinade from the container and discard it. Place the roast over the burner that is off. Close the grill's lid and cook the roast for 1 to 1½ hours, turning it once. The meat is done when a meat thermometer registers about 5 to 10 degrees shy of the desired temperature (140° F for rare, 160° F for medium, 170° F for well-done). A 4-to-6-pound chuck roast will take 1 to 1¼ hours to cook to the rare stage, 1¼ to 1¾ hours for medium, and 1¾ to 2 hours for well-done.

4. Transfer the roast to a carving board, cover it loosely with a foil tent, and let it rest for 10 minutes or so.

5. To serve, carve the meat on the diagonal into thin slices.

Serves 6 to 8

SAVORY SHORT RIBS OF BEEF

Anyone who really knows beef knows that short ribs are mighty fine eating, and usually quite a value at that. Put away the knives and forks—this is definitely a dish to eat with your hands.

MARINADE
½ cup dry red wine
¼ cup soy sauce
3 tablespoons vegetable oil
2 garlic cloves, pressed
¼ teaspoon dried thyme leaves
½ teaspoon fresh-ground black pepper

4 pounds short ribs

1. Combine all the marinade ingredients in a nonreactive container and mix well. Add the short ribs, submerge them in the marinade, cover the container, and refrigerate for 2 to 3 hours.

2. Preheat the grill for 10 to 15 minutes, with all the burners on high.

3. Once the grill is hot, turn one burner off and turn the other(s) to medium. Drain the marinade from the container and discard it. Position the short ribs over the burner that is off, close the grill's lid, and cook the meat for 1¼ to 1½ hours, turning the ribs every 10 to 15 minutes.

4. Serve the short ribs hot off the grill.

Serves 4 to 6

BASTED BEEF RIBS

Old-timers used to say: "The closer to the bone, the sweeter the meat." That's certainly the case with these ribs. You may have to request beef ribs from your butcher in advance, but they'll be worth the wait.

BASTING SAUCE
4 tablespoons paprika
2 tablespoons chili powder
2 tablespoons ground cumin
1 tablespoon ground oregano
1 tablespoon ground black pepper
1 tablespoon ground white pepper
1 teaspoon cayenne
2 tablespoons dark brown sugar
1 tablespoon sugar
2 tablespoons salt
½ cup cider vinegar
½ cup water
½ cup soy sauce
¼ cup Worcestershire sauce

4 pounds beef short ribs

1. To make the basting sauce, combine the spices, sugars, and salt in a nonreactive container and mix until thoroughly blended. Add the vinegar, water, soy sauce, and Worcestershire to the dry ingredients and mix well. About 30 minutes before grilling, brush the ribs with some of the basting sauce.

2. Preheat the grill for 10 to 15 minutes, with all the burners on high.

3. Once the grill is hot, turn one burner off and turn the other(s) to medium. Place the beef ribs over the burner that is off. Close the grill's lid and cook the ribs for about 60 minutes, turning them and basting with the sauce every 15 minutes or so.

4. Serve hot off the grill.

Serves 4 to 6

••◆••

GRILLED LIVER STEAKS

••◆••

Although liver is not to everyone's taste, you may be able to convert a few people with this recipe. Most liver lovers agree that medium is about as "done" as you want to cook liver; any more and it toughens and becomes dry. Serve with Grilled Onion Slices (page 186) and strips of crisp bacon. "Baked" Potatoes on the Grill (page 190) and a spinach salad also make wonderful companions.

1 pound liver steak (beef or calf), about 1 inch thick
3 tablespoons butter, melted
Salt and fresh-ground black pepper

1. Preheat the grill for 10 to 15 minutes, with all the burners on high.

2. While the grill is preheating, rub the liver steak with the melted butter and sprinkle it with salt and pepper.

3. Once the grill is hot, turn one burner off and turn the other(s) to medium. Position the liver over the burner that is off, close the grill's lid, and cook for about 15 to 20 minutes, turning the meat once or twice. Check for the desired degree of doneness by discreetly slicing into the liver steak with a sharp knife.

4. When the liver is done, slice it into individual portions and serve.

Serves 4

◆

PORK, HAM, AND SAUSAGE

◆

CHAPTER FIVE
PORK, HAM, AND SAUSAGE

•✦•

Barbecue purists may scoff at gas grills, but it is possible to get delicious pork barbecue from a gas grill. For the best-tasting barbecue, however, you may want to experiment with those wood chips you always thought you'd like to use someday. Soak the wood chips in warm water for about 30 minutes. Then place the chips in a small, disposable aluminum pan and cover with foil, or put them in a doubled piece of heavy-duty aluminum foil, folded over to make a secure packet. Pierce the foil in several places to allow the smoke to escape. The chips go over the burner(s) that remain on, while you cook the meat over the burner that is off. Keep the lid of the grill down and your pork will be bathed in delicious smoke.

Over the years, changes in tastes have influenced the types of pigs being bred. It was not long ago that huge, very fatty pigs were desirable. Today's pigs, however, are smaller and much leaner—yielding meat far lower in calories than that of old. A 3-ounce serving of a trimmed pork loin chop contains about 170 calories and about 7 grams of fat. (If you are watching calories and fat, be aware that the leanest pork cuts are the boneless pork loin roast and pork tenderloin.)

When buying pork, look for meat that is a pale, pinkish gray, with very white (not yellow) fat, and not too much of it. The darker the flesh, the older the animal.

Pork has become not only leaner, but also much more savory, because the recommended internal cooking temperature has been reduced. Fear of trichinosis caused generations of cooks to overcook pork, until it was dry and tasteless. The USDA has now determined that the parasite that causes trichinosis is destroyed instantly at 137° F. At 160° F—the point at which pork is done to the "medium" stage—there is absolutely no cause for concern regarding trichinosis. Pork cooked to medium may still be slightly pink, but the juices should run clear. Pork is considered well-done at 170° F.

As with all meats, remove pork from the refrigerator about 30 minutes before grilling, to allow the meat to come close to room temperature.

Wood chips add a delicious smoke flavor to grilled foods. Hickory adds the most intense flavor—it's great to use with pork. Other good wood choices are apple, cherry, maple, pecan, and walnut.

❖ AUTHENTIC BARBECUED SPARERIBS ❖

There's nothing much better than barbecued spareribs. The technique described in this recipe will produce the type of ribs you thought you could only get at a real barbecue joint. Allow 1 pound of ribs per person.

BASTING SAUCE
4 tablespoons paprika
2 tablespoons chili powder
2 tablespoons ground cumin
1 tablespoon ground oregano
1 tablespoon ground black pepper
1 tablespoon ground white pepper
2 teaspoons cayenne (optional)
2 tablespoons dark brown sugar
1 tablespoon sugar
2 tablespoons salt
½ cup cider vinegar
½ cup water
½ cup soy sauce
¼ cup Worcestershire sauce

2 slabs of pork ribs, full-slab or loin (a.k.a. baby back
*   ribs), about 4 to 6 pounds total*
Your favorite bottled barbecue sauce, heated

1. To make the basting sauce, combine the spices, sugars, and salt in a nonreactive bowl and mix thoroughly. Omit the cayenne if there are youngsters in the crowd, or if you or your guests don't care for spicy-hot food. Add the vinegar, water, soy sauce, and Worcestershire to the dry ingredients, mix well, and reserve.

2. About 30 minutes before grilling, remove the ribs from the refrigerator and brush them liberally with some of the basting sauce.

3. Preheat the grill for 10 to 15 minutes, with all the burners on high.

4. Once the grill is hot, turn one burner off and turn the other(s) to medium. Place the ribs over the burner that is off. Close the grill's lid and cook the ribs for 1½ hours, turning them every 20 minutes or so and basting them with the sauce.

5. Remove the ribs from the grill, cut the slab into individual ribs, and serve with your favorite bottled barbecue sauce (heated on the stove ahead of time) dribbled on top.

Serves 4 to 6

•◆•

CHINESE-STYLE SWEET AND SOUR PORK CHOPS

•◆•

The intense sweet and sour flavors typical of many Chinese sauces and marinades combine well with pork. Serve these chops with plenty of steamed rice, and perhaps some coleslaw made with Chinese cabbage and rice wine vinegar.

MARINADE
½ cup soy sauce
¼ cup hoisin sauce
¼ cup white vinegar
¼ cup honey
¼ cup pineapple juice
2 garlic cloves, pressed
3 tablespoons peanut or vegetable oil

6 pork loin or rib chops, each ¾ to 1 inch thick

1. Combine the marinade ingredients in a nonreactive container and mix well. Add the pork chops, cover the container, and refrigerate for 1 to 2 hours.

2. Preheat the grill for 10 to 15 minutes, with all the burners on high.

3. Once the grill is hot, turn one burner off and turn the other(s) to medium. Drain the marinade from the container and discard it. Place the pork chops over the burner that is off. Close the grill's lid and cook the chops for 25 to 30 minutes, turning them once.

4. Serve the pork chops hot off the grill.

Serves 6

SKEWERED MEXICAN PORK STRIPS

Marinated strips of pork tenderloin, grilled to succulent perfection, are the centerpiece for a "build-your-own-burrito" dinner. Folded inside a warm flour tortilla with Cowpoke Beans (page 224), tomato and avocado slices, and chopped red onion—not to mention your favorite hot sauce or salsa—this spicy skewered pork is a real hit.

MARINADE
⅓ cup fresh lime juice
⅓ cup apple juice
3 tablespoons vegetable oil
2 garlic cloves, pressed
1½ teaspoons chili powder
1 teaspoon ground cumin
1 teaspoon hot pepper sauce

2 pork tenderloins, each about ¾ to 1 pound
12 bamboo skewers, soaked in water

Flour tortillas
Tomato slices
Avocado slices
Diced red onion
Cowpoke Beans (page 224)
Sour cream (optional)
Hot sauce or salsa

1. Combine all the marinade ingredients in a nonreactive bowl and mix well. Cut the pork tenderloins lengthwise into ⅜-inch-thick strips. Cut the strips again lengthwise, into strips about ¾ to 1 inch wide. Cut these strips again, so that they are about 2½ inches long. Place the strips in the marinade, cover the container, and refrigerate for 2 to 4 hours.

2. Preheat the grill for 10 to 15 minutes, with all the burners on high.

3. While the grill is preheating, drain the marinade from the container into a nonreactive saucepan. Bring the liquid to a boil for

Meat thermometers are invaluable aids in all grilling. It's a good idea to keep a couple on hand, in case one breaks or disappears—a common occurrence.

a minute or two, remove the pan from the heat, and reserve for basting. Weave the marinated pork strips fairly tightly onto the skewers.

4. Once the grill is hot, turn one burner off and turn the other(s) to medium. Place the skewered pork over the burner that is off. Wrap the flour tortillas in foil and place them next to the pork. Close the grill's lid and cook the pork for 10 to 15 minutes, turning the skewers once and basting with the boiled marinade, if desired.

5. Assemble all the ingredients for the burritos, remove the skewered pork and the tortillas from the grill, and enjoy!

Serves 6 to 8

·•◆•·

CARIBBEAN SKEWERED PORK WITH GARLIC AND FRESH LIME

·•◆•·

Because of the intensity of the simple yet tasty marinade in this recipe, the pork need not marinate long. This dish is great for those occasions when you have little time but still want to serve something with lots of taste.

MARINADE
⅔ cup fresh lime juice
6 to 8 garlic cloves, pressed
⅓ cup vegetable oil

2 pork tenderloins, each about ¾ to 1 pound
12 bamboo skewers, soaked in water

1. Combine the marinade ingredients in a nonreactive container and mix well. Slice the pork into ¼-inch-thick strips, add the strips to the marinade, cover the container, and refrigerate for 30 minutes.

2. Preheat the grill for 10 to 15 minutes, with all the burners on high.

3. While the grill is preheating, drain the marinade from the container and discard it. Weave or thread the pork onto the skewers.

4. Once the grill is hot, turn one burner off and turn the other(s) to medium. Place the skewered pork over the burner that is off. Close the grill's lid and cook the pork for 10 to 15 minutes, turning the skewers once.

5. Serve the pork hot off the grill.

Serves 6 to 8

SKEWERED PORK WITH SPICY PEANUT MARINADE

My inspiration for this dish comes from the many excellent Thai dishes that feature peanuts and hot spices. This skewered pork recipe is both fast and delicious.

MARINADE
½ cup dry or medium-dry sherry
¼ cup soy sauce
¼ cup vegetable oil
2 to 4 garlic cloves, pressed
4 tablespoons peanut butter (chunky or smooth)
2 teaspoons dried red pepper flakes

2 pork tenderloins, each about ¾ to 1 pound
12 bamboo skewers, soaked in water

1. Combine the marinade ingredients in a nonreactive container and mix well. Slice the pork into ¼-inch-thick strips, add the strips to the marinade, cover the container, and refrigerate for 1 to 2 hours.

2. Preheat the grill for 10 to 15 minutes, with all the burners on high.

3. While the grill is preheating, drain the marinade from the container and discard it. Weave or thread the pork onto the skewers.

4. Once the grill is hot, turn one burner off and turn the other(s) to medium. Place the skewered pork over the burner that

is off. Close the grill's lid and cook the pork for 10 to 15 minutes, turning the skewers once.

5. Serve the pork hot off the grill.

Serves 6 to 8

•◆•

CURED PORK TENDERLOIN WITH RÉMOULADE SAUCE

•◆•

Don't let the word *cured* make you think that this recipe is difficult; it isn't. Curing a pork tenderloin makes the meat both firmer and more succulent. Read through the following instructions and you'll see just how easy it is. Slice the meat thin, serve it warm or cold with the rémoulade sauce, and you've got the perfect centerpiece for a big party buffet.

CURE
½ cup sugar
½ cup salt
8 cups water

2 pork tenderloins, each about ¾ to 1 pound
Vegetable oil
Fresh-ground black pepper

RÉMOULADE SAUCE
½ cup mayonnaise
3 tablespoons Dijon mustard
1 tablespoon chopped sweet pickle
1 tablespoon chopped capers
1 tablespoon chopped fresh parsley
½ teaspoon dried tarragon

1. The night before you plan to grill the pork, combine the cure ingredients in a container and stir to completely dissolve the sugar and salt. Add the tenderloins to the mixture, cover the container, and refrigerate overnight.

2. About 30 minutes before grilling time, remove the tenderloins from the cure, blot them as dry as you can, rub the meat with a little vegetable oil, and dust it with pepper.

3. Preheat the grill for 10 to 15 minutes, with all the burners on high.

4. While the grill is preheating, mix the rémoulade sauce ingredients in a bowl and refrigerate until serving time.

5. Once the grill is hot, turn one burner off and turn the other(s) to medium. Place the tenderloins over the burner that is off. Close the grill's lid and cook the meat for 25 to 35 minutes, turning it once or twice.

6. Transfer the tenderloins to a carving board, carve into thin slices, and serve with the rémoulade sauce on the side.

Serves 6 to 8

⋄•◆•⋄

PORK TENDERLOIN WITH DIJON MUSTARD GLAZE

⋄•◆•⋄

MARINADE
½ cup Dijon mustard
3 tablespoons extra-virgin olive oil
3 garlic cloves, pressed
¼ teaspoon fresh-ground pepper

2 pork tenderloins, each about ¾ to 1 pound

1. Combine all the marinade ingredients in a nonreactive container and mix well. Add the pork tenderloins to the container and turn the meat to coat it thoroughly with the marinade. Cover the container and refrigerate for 30 to 60 minutes.

2. Preheat the grill for 10 to 15 minutes, with all the burners on high.

3. Once the grill is hot, turn one burner off and turn the other(s) to medium. Drain the marinade from the container and discard it. Place the tenderloins over the burner that is off. Close the grill's lid and cook the meat for 25 to 35 minutes, turning it once or twice.

4. Transfer the tenderloins to a carving board, carve into thin slices, and serve.

Serves 6 to 8

∗∗◆∗∗
PORK TENDERLOIN BARBECUE
∗◆∗∗

This is a simple variation on that North Carolina specialty, the pulled pork sandwich. It makes an excellent center-piece for a buffet meal, along with warm hamburger buns, Not-Your-Mother's Coleslaw (page 220), and Homemade French Fries (page 227). This is a dish that everyone—even finicky youngsters—seems to love.

DRY RUB
4 tablespoons paprika
2 tablespoons chili powder
2 tablespoons ground cumin
1 tablespoon ground oregano
1 tablespoon ground black pepper
1 tablespoon ground white pepper
2 teaspoons cayenne (optional)
2 tablespoons salt
2 tablespoons dark brown sugar
1 tablespoon sugar

2 pork tenderloins, each about ¾ to 1 pound

Hamburger buns, warmed
Bottled barbecue sauce, heated
Dill pickle chips
Coleslaw

1. Combine all the dry rub ingredients in a shallow container and mix well. Omit the cayenne if you don't want the meat spicy-hot. Place the pork tenderloins in the container and cover with the

⋯⋯◆⋯⋯
Using dry spice rubs is one of the easiest and fastest ways to flavor any food for the grill.

dry rub, coating the meat thoroughly. Cover the container and re-frigerate for 2 to 4 hours.

2. Preheat the grill for 10 to 15 minutes, with all the burners on high.

3. Once the grill is hot, turn one burner off and turn the other(s) to medium. Remove the tenderloins from the container and place them over the burner that is off. Close the grill's lid and cook the meat for 25 to 35 minutes, turning it once or twice.

4. Transfer the tenderloins to a carving board and cut them in thin slices. Serve the slices on warm hamburger buns, topped with heated barbecue sauce, dill pickle chips, and some coleslaw.

Serves 6 to 8

⋄◆⋄ BURNT-END SANDWICHES ⋄◆⋄

Burnt-end sandwiches are indigenous to Kansas City, a town that takes its barbecue seriously. Most of the barbecue joints there serve some variation on the sandwich, most often cut from a barbecued beef brisket. Snead's, a long-time barbecue haven in Kansas City, developed the burnt-end sandwich into a culinary classic. It features toasted white bread, cut into triangles, topped with a few burnt-end pieces, some coleslaw, a couple of dill pickle chips and a squirt of barbecue sauce. Fold it over and . . . oh my—good eatin'!

In this version, we've replaced the brisket with a boneless pork loin rib-end roast, although boneless country-style ribs would also do nicely. The reason for this substitution is simple: pork loin ends are much smaller cuts of meat than the beef brisket, so it's easier to produce more burnt ends with them, not to mention that pork tends to be more succulent than beef.

BASTING SAUCE
4 tablespoons paprika
2 tablespoons chili powder
2 tablespoons ground cumin

1 tablespoon ground oregano
1 tablespoon ground black pepper
1 tablespoon ground white pepper
2 teaspoons cayenne (optional)
2 tablespoons dark brown sugar
1 tablespoon sugar
2 tablespoons salt
½ cup cider vinegar
½ cup water
½ cup soy sauce
¼ cup Worcestershire sauce

2-pound to 4-pound pork loin end roast

White bread, toasted
Dill pickle chips
Coleslaw
Barbecue sauce

1. To make the basting sauce, combine the spices, sugars, and salt in a nonreactive container and mix until thoroughly blended. Omit the cayenne if there are youngsters in the crowd, or if you or your guests don't care for spicy-hot food. Add the vinegar, water, soy sauce, and Worcestershire to the dry ingredients and mix well.

2. About 30 minutes before grilling, remove the pork from the refrigerator and brush it liberally with some of the basting sauce.

3. Preheat the grill for 10 to 15 minutes, with all the burners on high.

4. Once the grill is hot, turn one burner off and turn the other(s) to medium. Place the pork over the burner that is off. Close the grill's lid and cook the meat, without turning it, for 1½ to 2 hours. Baste the pork with the sauce every 20 minutes or so.

5. Transfer the pork to a carving board and cut the meat so that each piece has at least some burnt ends.

6. Serve the pork buffet style, letting each guest make a sandwich with the toast, pork, pickles, coleslaw, and barbecue sauce à la Snead's.

Serves 4 to 8

JAMAICAN JERKED PORK TENDERLOIN

Anyone who has traveled to Jamaica can tell you that jerk pork more than rivals Southern-style American barbecue. The flavors are intensely hot, sweet, and aromatic—all at the same time! I don't even try to replicate those flavors at home because I prefer the real stuff: jerk seasoning that has been bottled at the source, in Jamaica. If you can't find jerk seasoning, try my favorite: Walkerswood Jamaican Jerk Seasoning, from St. Ann, Jamaica, available via mail order from Le Saucier, Faneuil Hall Marketplace, Boston, Massachusetts 02109; 617-227-9649.

Bottled Jamaican jerk seasoning
Vegetable oil
2 pork tenderloins, each about ¾ to 1 pound

Chopped fresh cilantro, for garnish (optional)

1. Combine the jerk seasoning and the vegetable oil according to the label directions to make a paste-like marinade. Coat the tenderloins with the jerk seasoning "paste," cover them tightly, and refrigerate for 1 to 3 hours.

2. Preheat the grill for 10 to 15 minutes, with all the burners on high.

3. Once the grill is hot, turn one burner off and turn the other(s) to medium. Place the tenderloins over the burner that is off. Close the grill's lid and cook the meat for 25 to 35 minutes, turning it every 10 minutes or so.

4. Transfer the tenderloins to a carving board and slice them thin. Garnish the slices with cilantro, if desired, and serve.

Serves 6 to 8

After you've fin-
ished grilling the
last of your meal,
turn all the burn-
ers on high, close
the grill's lid, and
come back in
five to ten min-
utes. When you
return, any bits
of food that re-
mained will have
burned off, and
the grill will be
ready for next
time.

ROLLED PORK LOIN ROAST
FLORENTINE

This recipe was inspired by an Italian dish developed during the Renaissance. It's an impressive centerpiece to serve with Skewered Herbed Potatoes (page 191), Grilled Onion Slices (page 186), and some homemade chunky applesauce.

1 rolled boneless pork loin roast, about 3 to 5 pounds
¼ cup dried rosemary, crumbled
8 to 10 garlic cloves, peeled, each cut lengthwise into 4
* slivers*
Salt and fresh-ground black pepper
¼ cup olive oil

1. About an hour before you are ready to cook the pork roast, cut the string that holds the roast together and sprinkle 3 teaspoons of the crumbled rosemary, 8 or 10 of the garlic slivers, and the salt and pepper over the inside of the unrolled roast. Roll the roast back up and tie with fresh cotton string. Using the tip of a sharp knife, make as many incisions, evenly spaced around the roast, as you have garlic slivers left. Insert the garlic slivers into the incisions and rub the outside of the roast with olive oil. Sprinkle the remaining rosemary over the outside of the roast, pressing it in with the heel of your hand; dust with more salt and pepper. Cover the roast with plastic wrap and refrigerate until ready to grill.

2. Preheat the grill for 10 to 15 minutes, with all the burners on high.

3. Once the grill is hot, turn one burner off and turn the other(s) to medium. Place the pork roast over the burner that is off. Close the grill's lid and cook the meat for 1½ to 2½ hours, depending on the size of the roast. With a cut of meat this size, it's essential to use a meat thermometer. The roast will be cooked to medium (when the pork is at its most succulent) when it reaches 160° F, and cooked to well-done when it reaches 170° F. Once the roast has come within 10 degrees of the desired temperature, remove it from the grill.

4. Place the roast on a carving board and cover it loosely with a foil tent. Let the meat rest for 10 minutes or so, during which time the pork will continue to "cook" to the desired degree of doneness.

5. Cut the strings off the roast and carve the meat into fairly thin slices. Serve with any juices that may have accumulated on the carving board.

Serves 6 to 10

PORK LOIN NORMANDY

Apples and pork is a favorite combination from the Normandy region of France. Using thawed frozen apple juice concentrate in the marinade is a quick way to add intense apple flavor to the meat. Serve this dish with Sauerkraut-and-Potato Casserole (page 229).

1 rolled boneless pork loin roast, about 3 to 5 pounds

MARINADE
6-ounce can frozen apple juice concentrate, thawed
½ cup minced onion
½ cup dry white wine
3 tablespoons vegetable oil
2 tablespoons soy sauce
½ teaspoon dried rosemary, crumbled
Fresh-ground pepper to taste

1. Combine all the marinade ingredients in a nonreactive container and mix well. Add the pork roast, cover the container, and refrigerate for 2 to 4 hours.

2. Preheat the grill for 10 to 15 minutes, with all the burners on high.

3. Once the grill is hot, turn one burner off and turn the other(s) to medium. Drain the marinade from the container and discard it. Place the pork roast over the burner that is off. Close the grill's lid and cook the meat for 1½ to 1¾ hours, depending on the size of the roast. With a cut of meat this size, it's essential to use a meat thermometer. The roast will be cooked to medium (when the pork is at its most succulent) when it reaches 160° F, and cooked to well-done when it reaches 170° F. Once the roast has come within 10 degrees of the desired temperature, remove it from the grill.

4. Place the roast on a carving board and cover it loosely with a foil tent. Let the meat rest for 10 minutes or so, during which time the pork will continue to "cook" to the desired degree of doneness.

5. Cut the strings off the roast and carve the meat into fairly thin slices. Serve along with any juices that may have accumulated on the carving board.

Serves 6 to 10

WHOLE "FRESH HAM"

It's a mystery why the pork roast known as the fresh ham isn't served more often. As far as pork goes, it's probably the most flavorful and succulent cut there is. The whole fresh ham runs to 15 pounds, but it is most often offered at the meat counter cut in half, divided into the butt end and the shank end. Obviously, these are roasts to feed a crowd. Consider serving the meat with homemade applesauce, hominy, or the ever-popular mountain of mashed potatoes. The only seasoning a fresh ham requires is some salt and plenty of fresh-ground black pepper.

6-pound to 7-pound "fresh ham," butt or shank end
Salt and fresh-ground black pepper

1. Preheat the grill for 10 to 15 minutes, with all the burners on high.

2. While the grill is preheating, wipe the roast with a clean rag or paper towel and sprinkle liberally with salt and plenty of pepper.

3. Once the grill is hot, turn one burner off and turn the other(s) to medium. Place the fresh ham over the burner that is off. Close the grill's lid and cook for 3 to 4 hours, rotating the ham every hour or so. With a cut of meat this size, it's essential to use a meat thermometer. The fresh ham will be cooked to medium (when the pork is at its most succulent) when it reaches 160° F, and cooked to well-done when it reaches 170° F. Once the roast has come within 10 degrees of the desired temperature, remove it from the grill.

4. Place the roast on a carving board and cover it loosely with a foil tent. Let the meat rest for 10 minutes or so, during which time the pork will continue to "cook" to the desired degree of doneness.

5. Carve the meat into fairly thin slices. Serve along with any juices that may have accumulated on the carving board.

Serves 12 to 14

⬦

WHOLE CURED HAM ON THE GRILL

⬦

When you cook a ham on the grill, the object is not so much to "grill" it as it is to heat it, while imparting some of that smoky, outdoor flavor so difficult to achieve in an indoor oven. There's the added benefit, of course, of relieving some of the congestion in the kitchen—especially when there's already a hungry crowd assembled at your house for dinner.

GLAZE
½ cup soy sauce
2 teaspoons ground dried ginger
¼ cup sherry wine
¼ cup vegetable oil
2 garlic cloves, pressed
¼ cup real maple syrup or honey
1 teaspoon Tabasco sauce

10-pound to 15-pound fully cooked canned ham, or
    smoked and cured whole ham

1. Combine all the glaze ingredients in a bowl.

2. Preheat the grill for 10 to 15 minutes, with all the burners on high.

3. Once the grill is hot, turn one burner off and turn the other(s) to medium. Place the ham over the burner that is off, fat side up. Close the grill's lid and cook the ham for 15 to 18 minutes per pound, or until a meat thermometer inserted into the center of the ham registers 140° F. Cook a smoked and cured ham to 160° F, because it has not been fully precooked (if the ham is fully precooked, it will say so; if you have any doubt, ask your butcher). Rotate the ham every half hour or so. Baste liberally with the glaze during the last 30 minutes of cooking.

4. Transfer the ham to a carving board, cover it loosely with a foil tent, and let it rest for 15 minutes.

5. Carve the ham thin and serve.

Serves 20 to 30

•◆•

HAM STEAKS WITH GRILLED FRESH PINEAPPLE SPEARS

•◆•

A big ham steak is one of the easiest and tastiest foods you can cook on the grill. It's a real crowd pleaser, because it's hard to find anyone, including youngsters, who dislikes the taste of ham. Combine this dish with Grilled Fresh Pineapple Spears (page 213) and you've got the makings of a memorable meal.

MARINADE
¼ cup soy sauce
1 teaspoon ground dried ginger
2 tablespoons dry sherry
2 tablespoons vegetable oil
2 garlic cloves, pressed
2 tablespoons real maple syrup or honey
1 teaspoon Tabasco sauce

1 ham steak, about 1 inch thick
Grilled Fresh Pineapple Spears

1. Combine all the marinade ingredients in a nonreactive container and mix well. Add the ham steak, turn it to coat it well, cover the container, and refrigerate for 30 to 60 minutes.

•◆•

To keep ham steaks from curling on the grill, cut slashes through the fat around the edges at 1-inch intervals.

2. Preheat the grill for 10 to 15 minutes, with all the burners on high.

3. Once the grill is hot, turn one burner off and turn the other(s) to medium. Remove the ham steak from the marinade and place it over the burner that is off. Close the grill's lid and cook the ham for 12 minutes, turning it once and basting with the leftover marinade.

4. When the ham is heated through, transfer it to a warm serving platter, surrounded by the grilled fresh pineapple spears, and serve. Your family will love you.

Serves 3 to 4

•◆•

CHINESE-STYLE PORK BURGERS

•◆•

As unusual as these "hamburgers" are, it's amazing how quickly people take to them. Be sure to toast the buns on the grill before serving the burgers.

1 pound lean ground pork
1 egg, beaten
¼ cup fine dry breadcrumbs
2 tablespoons minced green onions (white part only)
1 garlic clove, pressed
½ teaspoon salt
½ teaspoon fresh-ground pepper

4 hamburger buns
Hoisin sauce
Green onions, cut in half lengthwise, and then cut into
*   1-inch pieces*
Bean sprouts

1. Combine the ground pork, beaten egg, breadcrumbs, onion, garlic, and salt and pepper in a bowl. Mix well, using your hands. Shape the mixture into 4 patties, each about ¾ inch thick. Refrigerate the patties until grilling time.

2. Preheat the grill for 10 to 15 minutes, with all the burners on high.

3. Once the grill is hot, turn all the burners to medium. With the grill's lid open, cook the pork patties for a total of 14 to 18 minutes, turning them once. The pork patties will be done when the juices run clear.

4. A couple of minutes before the pork patties are done, put the buns on the grill to warm.

5. Place one patty in each bun, top with a tablespoon or so of hoisin sauce, sprinkle with green onion slivers and bean sprouts, and serve.

Serves 4

BRATWURST IN BEER

This is a good recipe for an informal get-together: it's easy, inexpensive, and tasty. Serve the bratwurst on good-quality buns, with plenty of sauerkraut, chopped onions, and a variety of mustards. German potato salad and steamed green beans, served at room temperature, dressed with a simple oil-and-vinegar vinaigrette, make excellent side dishes.

Two 12-ounce cans beer
12 bratwurst

1. Preheat the grill for 10 to 15 minutes, with all the burners on high.

2. Once the grill is hot, turn one burner off and turn the other(s) to medium. Place a disposable aluminum roasting pan over the burner that is off and pour the beer into the pan.

3. Position the sausage over the burner that is on. Close the grill's lid and cook the bratwurst for 10 to 12 minutes, turning the sausages frequently, until they are lightly browned.

4. As they brown, move the bratwurst into the pan with the beer. Once all the sausages are in the pan, close the grill's lid and cook them for another 20 to 25 minutes.

5. Serve the bratwurst directly from the pan. Leave any left-overs in the pan, so that the last brat will be as hot and juicy as the first; they won't stay left over for long!

Serves 6 to 8

‡◆‡

GRILLED BOCKWURST WITH SAUERKRAUT, APPLESAUCE, AND CORNBREAD

‡◆‡

When teamed with sauerkraut, applesauce, and cornbread hot from the oven, bockwurst—mild white sausages made from pork and veal—makes an excellent cool-weather meal. Store-bought sauerkraut and applesauce are both excellent products, and the packaged cornbread mixes rival the homemade versions. So the only real cooking involved in this meal is to simply grill the sausages and bake the cornbread!

8 bockwurst
2 pounds sauerkraut, heated
Applesauce
Cornbread
A variety of mustards

1. Preheat the grill for 10 to 15 minutes, with all the burners on high.

2. Once the grill is hot, turn one burner off and turn the other(s) to medium. Position the sausage over the burner that is off. Close the grill's lid and cook for 12 to 18 minutes, turning them frequently, until the sausages are lightly browned.

3. Place the grilled bockwurst on top of the hot sauerkraut and serve with applesauce on the side, a basket of cornbread, and a variety of mustards.

Serves 4

Keep plenty of aluminum foil nearby when you're grilling, especially the heavy-duty variety; it can be a griller's best friend.

✦

SAUSAGE-AND-CHEESE QUESADILLAS

✦

The addition of chorizo sausage turns these quesadillas into a hearty main dish.

1 pound uncooked chorizo sausage
8 large flour tortillas
1 tablespoon vegetable oil
4 cups grated Monterey jack or mild cheddar cheese (or a
*   combination of both)*
Salsa (optional)
Chopped fresh cilantro, for garnish (optional)

1. Remove the chorizo from the casings. Crumble the sausage into a skillet and sauté over medium heat for 15 to 30 minutes. Remove the sausage from the skillet using a slotted spoon and drain it on several layers of paper towel.

2. While the sausage is cooking, preheat the grill for 10 to 15 minutes, with all the burners on high.

3. While the grill is preheating, assemble the quesadillas. Lightly brush one side of each tortilla with vegetable oil. Place 4 tortillas, oiled side down, side by side on your work surface. Divide the cheese among the 4 tortillas and layer evenly. Sprinkle the chorizo on top. Top each circle with another tortilla, this time with the oiled side facing up. Press down lightly on each quesadilla to compress the cheese and sausage.

4. Once the grill is hot, turn all the burners to low. Using a spatula, carefully place the quesadillas on the grill. Watch closely: as soon as the cheese begins to melt, turn each quesadilla over and brown the other side. The quesadillas are done when they are lightly toasted on both sides and the cheese is completely melted.

5. Cut the quesadillas into wedges and serve warm. If desired, top them with your favorite hot sauce or salsa, or sprinkle them with cilantro.

Serves 4

GRILLED ITALIAN SAUSAGES WITH POLENTA

Depending on your diners' tastes, choose hot or mild Italian sausage. If you haven't tried it, try to find a brand of "instant" polenta that cooks in five minutes, which is every bit as good as the regular polenta and takes a lot less time and effort. This dish goes exceptionally well with spinach sautéed with garlic in olive oil and splashed with a little balsamic vinegar.

½ recipe Polenta (page 233)
8 Italian sausages, hot or mild

1. Cook the polenta according to the recipe directions. Keep the mixture warm on a large platter, covered with foil, in a 225° F oven.

2. Preheat the grill for 10 to 15 minutes, with all the burners on high.

3. Once the grill is hot, turn one burner off and turn the other(s) to medium. Position the sausages over the burner that is off. Close the grill's lid and cook the links for 15 to 20 minutes, turning them frequently, until they are browned.

4. Place the grilled Italian sausage on top of, or around the sides of, the polenta. Serve hot.

Serves 4

CHAPTER SIX

◆

LAMB AND VEAL

◆

CHAPTER SIX
LAMB AND VEAL

•◆•

Although lamb and veal aren't quite as popular for grilling as beef and pork, many cuts are greatly enhanced by grilling. Just remember to treat these tender meats with care: overcooked lamb or veal is tough.

As with all meats, be sure to remove the lamb or veal from the refrigerator about 30 minutes before grilling.

LAMB

..◆..

According to the USDA, lamb labeled "genuine lamb," "lamb," or "spring lamb" must be less than one year old. Sheep that are between one and two years old are classified as "yearlings." Furthermore, the term *spring lamb* identifies lamb processed between the first Monday in March and the first Monday in October. In general, the paler the meat, the younger the lamb—and the more tender.

A special program administered by the USDA encourages ranchers to raise leaner lamb. After being graded by USDA inspectors, this special lamb is given a red, white, and blue sticker, proclaiming it as "Certified Fresh American Lamb." About the top third of lamb produced in this country receives this designation. Domestic lamb, which is usually grain-fed, tends to be more tender than imported, grass-fed lamb.

There is often a thin, parchment-like membrane called a "fell" covering the fat on lamb. The butcher usually removes it from chops, but you'll find it covering larger cuts. Don't remove the fell, because it helps keep the meat from drying out.

Because lamb is so tender, it is very tasty served rare. Remember that lamb, like all meats, continues to cook after it is taken off the grill. Remove lamb, especially large cuts such as roasts, when its internal temperature registers approximately 10 degrees shy of the desired temperature. Place the meat on a carving board, cover it loosely with a foil tent, and let it rest for 10 to 15 minutes before carving. The resting period allows the meat not only to reach the level of doneness you desire, but also to reabsorb the flavorful juices, yielding a more succulent dish.

Lamb is considered rare at 140° F, medium at 160° F, and well-done at 170° F.

◆

Roasts are often considered "company's-coming" food, special-occasion food that's difficult to cook. In truth, a roast is one of the easiest foods to cook: simply season it, put it on the grill, cook it until it reaches the desired temperature, and slice it. That's it!

VEAL

⬩◆⬩

T he most delicate veal comes from milk-fed calves, butchered when they are between eight and twelve weeks old. The meat is pale pink and the fat (of which there should be little) is satiny white. A lower grade of veal, but still a good one, comes from grass-fed calves, usually butchered when they are four or five months old. The meat is darker pink than that of milk-fed veal, but it should never be red.

Veal is considered rare at 140° F and medium at 160° F; because veal is so lean, it should never be cooked well-done. Most chefs aim for an internal temperature of about 150° F, or medium-rare.

⬩◆⬩

LAMB CHOPS WITH MINT SAUCE

⬩◆⬩

F or those of us brought up on well-done lamb and store-bought mint jelly, serving lamb medium-rare with an authentic mint sauce will come as a pleasant change. Not overcooking the lamb greatly benefits its flavor, and a piquant, minty sauce is, for most people, quite an improvement over mint jelly.

MINT SAUCE
2 tablespoons minced fresh mint
1 tablespoon brown sugar
½ cup white wine vinegar

Olive oil
8 lamb loin chops
Salt and fresh-ground black pepper

1. Combine the mint sauce ingredients in a small, lidded jar. Shake well. Taste the sauce and adjust the amounts of vinegar and sugar, if you desire.

2. Preheat the grill for 10 to 15 minutes, with all the burners on high.

3. While the grill is preheating, rub a little olive oil on both sides of each chop, and dust each one with salt and pepper.

4. Once the grill is hot, turn all the burners to medium. With the grill's lid open, cook the chops for 10 to 14 minutes, turning them once. This cooking time will yield chops cooked to medium; adjust the time slightly if you desire a different degree of doneness.

5. Serve the chops hot off the grill, passing the mint sauce at the table.

Serves 4

⁺∙◆∙⁺
LAMB CHOPS WITH FRESH DILL SAUCE
⁺∙◆∙⁺

The flavors of lamb and fresh dill do wonderful things for each other. This outstanding dish is just the thing when you're trying to impress your guests. Serve with Skewered Herbed Potatoes (page 191) and fresh asparagus.

DILL SAUCE
2 tablespoons butter
2 tablespoons minced shallots
⅓ cup dry white wine
2 tablespoons minced fresh dill
¼ teaspoon salt
⅓ cup heavy cream

Olive oil
8 lamb loin chops
Salt and fresh-ground black pepper
Dill sprigs, for garnish (optional)

1. To make the dill sauce, melt the butter in a small saucepan. Add the shallots and sauté over medium heat until they are soft, about 3 minutes. Add the white wine, bring the mixture to a boil, and then reduce the heat to low. Add the dill and the salt, and slowly drizzle in the cream. Let the sauce simmer (do not let it boil) for

5 to 10 minutes, stirring it constantly. Remove the pan from the heat and reserve until serving time.

2. Preheat the grill for 10 to 15 minutes, with all the burners on high.

3. While the grill is preheating, rub a little olive oil on both sides of each chop, and dust each one with salt and pepper.

4. Once the grill is hot, turn all the burners to medium. With the grill's lid open, cook the chops for 10 to 14 minutes, turning them once. This cooking time will yield chops cooked to medium; adjust the time slightly if you desire a different degree of doneness.

5. While the chops are on the grill, gently reheat the dill sauce. Do not let it come to a boil.

6. Serve the chops hot off the grill with a little dill sauce drizzled on top. Pass additional sauce at the table. Garnish the chops with sprigs of fresh dill, if desired.

Serves 4

⁺⁺◆⁺⁺

MARINATED GREEK LAMB SHOULDER CHOPS

⁺⁺◆⁺⁺

Lamb shoulder (or sirloin) chops cook up beautifully on a gas grill. The Greek marinade adds a wonderful dimension to the lamb, especially good when served with a Greek salad.

MARINADE
¾ cup dry white or rosé wine
¼ cup extra-virgin olive oil
6 bay leaves
1 small onion, minced
4 garlic cloves, pressed
8 lemon peel strips (yellow part only), each about 1 inch long
3 teaspoons dried oregano, crumbled

4 lamb shoulder or sirloin chops, each about 1 inch thick

1. Combine all the marinade ingredients in a small saucepan and bring the mixture to a boil. Remove the pan from the heat and let the marinade cool to room temperature. Place the lamb chops in a large, shallow, nonreactive dish, cover them with the cooled mari-nade, cover the dish, and refrigerate for 4 to 6 hours, or overnight if desired.

2. Preheat the grill for 10 to 15 minutes, with all the burners on high.

3. Once the grill is hot, turn all the burners to medium. Drain the marinade from the dish and discard it. With the grill's lid open, cook the chops for 10 to 16 minutes, turning them once. This cook-ing time will yield chops cooked to medium; adjust the time slight-ly if you desire a different degree of doneness.

4. Serve the lamb chops hot off the grill.

Serves 4

MEDITERRANEAN LAMB SHISH KEBOBS

It's hard to go wrong with lamb shish kebobs, marinated and grilled to order. An excellent choice as a dinner-party main course, the lamb kebobs can be paired up with a rice pilaf and Marinated Eggplant with Tomatoes and Fontina Cheese (page 177). First-class dining!

MARINADE
½ cup extra-virgin olive oil
¼ cup dry white wine
2 tablespoons red wine vinegar
4 garlic cloves, pressed
1 tablespoon dried rosemary
1 teaspoon dried thyme leaves
2 teaspoons fresh-ground black pepper

2 pounds boneless lamb, cut into 1¼-inch cubes
12 bamboo skewers, soaked in water

1. Combine all the marinade ingredients in a nonreactive container and mix well. Add the cubed lamb to the marinade, toss the cubes to coat them, cover the container, and refrigerate for 4 to 6 hours, or overnight if desired.

2. Preheat the grill for 10 to 15 minutes, with all the burners on high.

3. While the grill is preheating, drain the marinade from the container and discard it. Thread the lamb cubes onto the skewers.

4. Once the grill is hot, turn all the burners to low. With the grill's lid closed, cook the lamb over direct heat for about 20 minutes, turning the skewers once or twice. This cooking time will yield lamb cooked to medium; adjust the time slightly if you desire a different degree of doneness.

5. Serve the shish kebobs hot off the grill.

Serves 6

•◆•

LAMB SOUVLAKI BURGERS

•◆•

Here's the Greek version of the American hamburger: seasoned ground lamb patties, grilled, slipped inside warm pita bread, and topped off with a tangy yogurt-cucumber sauce (known as *tzatziki*). For a cheese-souvlaki-burger, add a little crumbled feta cheese inside the pita.

TZATZIKI SAUCE
½ cup plain yogurt
¼ cup peeled, seeded, and chopped cucumber
½ teaspoon dried dill
½ teaspoon dried mint leaves, crumbled

1½ pounds ground lamb
¼ onion, minced
2 teaspoons dried oregano, crumbled
1 teaspoon salt
2 teaspoons fresh-ground black pepper

4 regular-size pita breads
1 cup shredded lettuce
1 large tomato, chopped
4 green onions, chopped

1. Combine all the *tzatziki* sauce ingredients in a bowl and mix well. Refrigerate the sauce until serving time.

2. In a large bowl, combine the ground lamb, onion, oregano, salt, and pepper. Using your hands, mix the ingredients thoroughly. Shape the mixture into 4 oval patties, each about ¾ inch thick.

3. Preheat the grill for 10 to 15 minutes, with all the burners on high.

4. While the grill is preheating, open the pita pockets, so they will be ready for the lamb patties.

5. Once the grill is hot, turn all the burners to medium. With the grill's lid open, cook the lamb patties for 14 to 18 minutes, turning them once. This cooking time will yield patties cooked to medium; adjust the time slightly if you desire a different degree of doneness.

6. A couple of minutes before the lamb patties are done, put the pita breads on the grill to warm.

7. To serve, put one patty in each pita bread, add the lettuce, tomato, and onion, and top with the *tzatziki* sauce.

Serves 4

ROAST LEG OF LAMB WITH WHITE BEANS

The combination of roast leg of lamb and white beans is a favorite in French households, particularly in Normandy. If you or your family and friends prefer a lamb with a flavor that's not so strong, have your butcher trim the leg of all its fat. Compensate for the loss of fat by rubbing the leg with softened butter.

4-pound to 6-pound leg of lamb
2 garlic cloves, peeled and cut into 8 slivers total
*3 tablespoons butter, softened (if the leg has been
    trimmed of fat)*
Salt and fresh-ground black pepper
Chopped fresh parsley, for garnish (optional)

WHITE BEANS
3 tablespoons olive oil
1 medium onion, minced
1 medium carrot, minced
*Two 15-ounce cans small white beans, drained and
    rinsed*
1 can chicken or vegetable stock
2 to 3 large garlic cloves, pressed
1 bay leaf
1 teaspoon dried thyme leaves
1 teaspoon salt
½ teaspoon fresh-ground black pepper

1. Preheat the grill for 10 to 15 minutes, with all the burners on high.

2. While the grill is preheating, use the point of a sharp knife to make 8 incisions, deep enough to hold the garlic, across the top of the leg of lamb. Insert a garlic sliver into each incision. If the leg has been trimmed of fat, rub the softened butter on the lamb. Sprinkle the lamb with salt and pepper.

3. Once the grill is hot, turn one burner off and turn the other(s) to medium. Place the lamb over the burner that is off. Close the grill's lid and cook the leg of lamb, rotating it every half-hour or so, for 2 to 2½ hours. This cooking time yields a leg of lamb cooked to medium, or 160° F. If you want a different degree of doneness, adjust the cooking time accordingly. The desired internal temperatures for lamb are 140° F for rare, 160° F for medium, and 170° F for well-done. Be sure to use a meat thermometer, inserted deep into the meat, to measure the internal temperature. Remove the leg from the grill when the thermometer registers 10 degrees shy of the desired temperature.

4. While the lamb cooks, prepare the white beans. In a large saucepan, heat the olive oil over medium-high heat. Add the onion and carrot, and sauté until the onion is soft and transparent, about

Remember that all food continues to cook after it is taken off the grill. Your best bet is to remove it when it is just shy of the desired degree of doneness.

4 minutes. Add the beans, chicken or vegetable stock, garlic, and the seasonings. Bring the mixture to a boil and then simmer it, uncovered, for about 20 minutes, stirring the beans occasionally. When done, the beans should be neither too soupy nor too thick. Remove the pan from heat.

5. Transfer the leg of lamb to a carving board, and cover it loosely with a foil tent. Let the lamb rest for 10 minutes or so; it will continue to "cook" to the desired degree of doneness. Meanwhile, reheat the beans, adding more stock, if necessary, to maintain the right consistency.

6. To serve, carve the lamb into fairly thin slices. Arrange slices on a serving platter along with the white beans; pour any juices that may have accumulated on the carving board over the sliced lamb and beans. Garnish with a little parsley, if desired.

Serves 6 to 8

GREEK BUTTERFLIED LEG OF LAMB WITH LEMON AND OREGANO

An exceptional dish to serve to a crowd, a butterflied leg of lamb is easy to grill, easy to carve, and with its special marinade, especially flavorful. It goes great with Garlicky Grilled Tomatoes (page 196) and Rosemary Potato Wedges (page 192). *Note:* It takes time to properly butterfly a leg of lamb, so order it from your butcher in advance.

MARINADE
¾ cup dry white or rosé wine
¼ cup extra-virgin olive oil
6 bay leaves
1 small onion, minced
4 garlic cloves, pressed
8 lemon peel strips (yellow part only), each about 1 inch long
1 tablespoon dried oregano, crumbled

4-pound to 6-pound leg of lamb, boned, trimmed, and butterflied

1. Combine all the marinade ingredients in a small saucepan and bring the mixture to a boil. Remove the pan from the heat and let the marinade cool to room temperature. Place the butterflied leg of lamb in a nonreactive container, pour the marinade over it, cover the container, and refrigerate for 4 to 6 hours, or overnight if desired.

2. Preheat the grill for 10 to 15 minutes, with all the burners on high.

3. While the grill is preheating, drain the marinade from the container into a nonreactive saucepan. Bring the marinade to a boil, remove the pan from the heat, and reserve the mixture for basting.

4. Once the grill is hot, turn one burner off and turn the other(s) to medium. Place the lamb over the burner that is off. Close the grill's lid and cook the lamb for 45 to 55 minutes for rare (140° F), 55 to 65 minutes for medium (160° F), or 1¼ hours for well-done (170° F). Turn the lamb several times during the cooking process, basting it with the boiled marinade. Remove the meat from the grill when it is 10 degrees shy of the desired internal temperature.

5. Transfer the lamb to a carving board, cover it loosely with a foil tent, and let it rest for 10 minutes or so.

6. To serve, carve the lamb into fairly thin slices. Arrange the slices on a serving platter, and pour any juices that may have accumulated on the carving board over the sliced lamb.

Serves 6 to 8

•◆•

GARLIC-AND-ROSEMARY RACK OF LAMB

•◆•

This rack of lamb, infused with the classic combination of garlic and rosemary, is very easy to grill to perfection—and it never fails to make a memorable impression. *Note:* When you purchase the lamb, ask your butcher to make a cut for the garlic and rosemary along the length of each rack, between the meat and the rib bones, but not all the way through to the other side.

2 racks of lamb, each about 1½ to 1¾ pounds
4 to 6 garlic cloves, pressed
1 tablespoon dried rosemary, crumbled
Salt and fresh-ground black pepper
Olive oil

1. Preheat the grill for 10 to 15 minutes, with all the burners on high.

2. While the grill is preheating, spread the garlic, rosemary, salt, and pepper in the openings between the meat and the rib bones in each rack, making an even layer with your fingers. Rub a little olive oil over the outside of each rack; dust the lamb with more salt and pepper.

3. Once the grill is hot, turn one burner off and turn the other(s) to medium. Place the racks of lamb over the burner that is off. Close the grill's lid and cook the lamb for 60 minutes for rare (140° F), 1 hour and 20 minutes for medium (160° F), or 1 hour and 30 minutes for well-done (170° F). Turn the racks several times during the cooking process. Remove the meat from the grill when it is 10 degrees shy of the desired internal temperature.

4. Place the lamb on a carving board, cover it loosely with a foil tent, and let it rest for 10 minutes or so.

5. Carve the racks into individual rib chops. Arrange the slices on a serving platter, pour any juices that may have accumulated on the carving board over the chops, and serve.

Serves 4

·◆·◆·◆·

GRILLED VEAL CHOPS WITH LEMON-CAPER SAUCE

·◆·◆·◆·

Veal chops and the grill were made for each other. Chops cook up quickly and, with the addition of a zesty lemon-caper sauce, are special enough to serve for a dinner party.

LEMON-CAPER SAUCE
¼ cup butter
1 tablespoon fresh lemon juice
1 tablespoon capers, or more to taste, rinsed

4 veal chops, each about 1 inch thick
Olive oil
Fresh-ground black pepper

1. To make the lemon-caper sauce, melt the butter in a small saucepan. Remove the pan from the heat and let the butter cool partially. Stir in the lemon juice and capers, and set aside until serving time.

2. About 30 minutes before grilling, rub the chops with olive oil and dust them liberally with pepper.

3. Preheat the grill for 10 to 15 minutes, with all the burners on high.

4. Once the grill is hot, sear the chops by placing them directly over the heat (with the burners still on high) and close the grill's lid. Sear only one side of each chop, for about 2 minutes for 1-inch chops. After searing the chops on one side, turn one burner off and turn the other(s) to medium. Flip the chops over (so the seared side is up), move them directly over the burner that is off, and close the grill's lid. Finish cooking the chops by the indirect method, turning them once. After searing, 1-inch chops will take 4 to 5 minutes to cook to rare and 5 to 7 minutes to cook to medium; cooking veal to well-done is not recommended, because the meat will be very dry. Meanwhile, warm the lemon-caper sauce, if desired.

5. Serve the lamb hot off the grill, topped with the lemon-caper sauce.

Serves 4

·······◆·······

It's a good idea to keep a spare tank of gas for your grill on hand. You'll thank yourself the day you run out of gas after all the stores have closed. Be sure to store the extra tank outdoors, in a safe location, where the temperature will never exceed 125° F.

VEAL CHOPS WITH BASIL-MUSTARD SAUCE

BASIL-MUSTARD SAUCE
1 tablespoon butter
2 tablespoons minced shallots
½ cup chicken stock
20 large fresh basil leaves, minced
1½ teaspoons Dijon mustard
⅓ cup heavy cream

4 veal chops, each about 1 inch thick
Olive oil
Fresh-ground black pepper

1. To make the basil-mustard sauce, melt the butter in a small saucepan. Add the shallots and sauté over medium heat until they are soft. Pour in the chicken stock and bring the mixture to a boil. Reduce the heat, and stir in the basil, mustard, and cream. Let the sauce simmer for 5 to 10 minutes (do not let it boil). Remove the pan from the heat and reserve until serving time.

2. About 30 minutes before grilling, rub the chops with olive oil and dust them liberally with pepper.

3. Preheat the grill for 10 to 15 minutes, with all the burners on high.

4. Once the grill is hot, sear the chops by placing them directly over the heat (with the burners still on high) and close the grill's lid. Sear only one side of each chop, for about 2 minutes for 1-inch chops. After searing the chops on one side, turn one burner off and turn the other(s) to medium. Flip the chops over (so the seared side is up), move them directly over the burner that is off, and close the grill's lid. Finish cooking the chops by the indirect method, turning them once. After searing, 1-inch chops will take 4 to 5 minutes to cook to rare and 5 to 7 minutes to cook to medium; cooking veal to well-done is not recommended, because the meat will be very dry. Meanwhile, warm the basil-mustard sauce over low heat.

5. Serve the chops hot off the grill, topped with the basil-mustard sauce.

Serves 4

◆

VEGETABLES AND VEGETARIAN MAIN DISHES

◆

Chapter Seven
Vegetables and Vegetarian Main Dishes

•⋄◆⋄•

Homegrown vegetables are naturally good in soups, casseroles, stews, and other kitchen fare, but they are even better hot off the grill. After all, both garden and grill are outdoors. And grilling, the simplest (not to mention the oldest) form of cooking, perfectly suits the ripe flavors of freshly harvested vegetables.

One primary reason most people grow their own vegetables is for the superior flavor of homegrown produce. If that's the case for you, experiment on your grill with all manner of vegetables. You'll find that they need no masking with heavy sauces, no transformation of taste or texture with extra-long cooking times.

Gas grills may not impart the rustic smokiness associated with charcoal grilling, but their consistency of temperature and clean-burning qualities are ideal for cooking vegetables— some would say even better than a charcoal grill.

The following are a few general guidelines for successfully preparing vegetables on the grill:

• With the exception of onions and eggplant (and there are many who would omit eggplant from the list), there's no need to peel vegetables for the grill. Potatoes and carrots easily come clean if you use one of those tough plastic scrubbing pads.

• Vegetables with many layers, such as onions and fennel, are best quartered, leaving some of the stem end intact. Doing so keeps the layers from separating into a lot of hard-to-manage pieces.

• Resist the temptation to parboil or partially cook in the microwave oven any vegetable before grilling. Both techniques alter the texture of the vegetable, resulting in a mushy, inferior dish.

• Skewered small, round vegetables, such as pearl onions, zucchini rounds, and cherry tomatoes, are the devil to keep from twirling around as you turn the skewers on the grill. Your best bet is to thread the vegetables on two pre-soaked bamboo skewers, parallel to one another; it works like a charm.

·•◆•·
MARINATED GRILLED ASPARAGUS
·•◆•·

Yes, asparagus can be grilled. The trick, of course, is to keep them perpendicular, rather than parallel, to the grill bars. With that caveat, grilling asparagus is strongly recommended; they're quite different in flavor and texture from the steamed version, and very tasty.

> *2 pounds fresh asparagus, the fatter the better*
> *1 cup homemade or commercial bottled vinaigrette*
>   *dressing*
> *Mayonnaise or lemon juice (optional)*

1. Preheat the grill for 10 to 15 minutes, with all the burners on high.

2. While the grill is preheating, wash the asparagus under cold water. Using a vegetable peeler, scrape off the skin from the bottom third of each asparagus spear. With a sharp knife, trim off the tough bottom ½ inch or so from each spear.

3. In a nonreactive container, combine the asparagus and vinaigrette. Let the vegetables sit briefly, about 10 minutes.

4. Once the grill is hot, turn one burner off and turn the other(s) to medium. Drain the marinade from the container; put the vinaigrette aside to serve at the table, if you wish. Position the asparagus over the burner that is off, close the grill's lid, and cook the vegetables for 5 to 8 minutes, turning them once or twice.

5. Serve the asparagus warm off the grill, with a little mayonnaise, lemon juice, or some of the leftover vinaigrette, if desired.

Serves 4 to 6

As a rule, never precook any fruit or vegetables before grilling: the food will lose both flavor and texture in the process.

BUTTERED GRILLED CARROTS

To many a mind, carrots are best when grilled. There's something about the grilling process and the dry heat that enhances the carrot's natural texture and flavor. Grilled carrots are excellent served with the Fresh Ginger–Orange Sauce from the next recipe, or simply buttered lightly and sprinkled with minced parsley.

> *4 to 8 large carrots (the larger the better)*
> *About ¼ cup butter, melted*
> *Minced fresh parsley (optional)*

1. Preheat the grill for 10 to 15 minutes, with all the burners on high.

2. While the grill is preheating, cut the tops from the carrots and scrub the carrots under cold water; do not peel them. Blot the carrots dry and then coat them liberally with the melted butter.

3. Once the grill is hot, turn one burner off and turn the other(s) to medium. Position the carrots over the burner that is off, close the grill's lid, and cook the carrots for 20 to 30 minutes, turning them occasionally. The carrots will be done when the tip of a sharp knife easily pierces them at their thickest part.

4. Serve the carrots hot off the grill with a little extra melted butter and a sprinkling of parsley, if desired.

Serves 4

GRILLED WHOLE BEETS WITH FRESH GINGER–ORANGE SAUCE

The flavor combination of oranges, ginger, and beets is outstanding. Grating the ginger with the skin intact and then squeezing it with your hands releases an amazing amount of ginger "juice"—an easy way to get the essence of this special rhizome.

FRESH GINGER–ORANGE SAUCE
2 tablespoons mayonnaise
4 tablespoons fresh orange juice
¼ teaspoon salt
½ cup grated unpeeled ginger

2 pounds beets (select the largest beets you can find—
  each at least as big as a tennis ball)

1. To make the sauce, combine the mayonnaise, orange juice, and salt in a nonreactive container. Using your hands, gather the grated ginger together in a ball and squeeze it tightly over the mayonnaise mixture. Discard the grated ginger. Stir the sauce, and refrigerate until serving time.

2. Preheat the grill for 10 to 15 minutes, with all the burners on high.

3. While the grill is preheating, scrub the beets. Cut the tops and roots from the beets, but do not peel them.

4. Once the grill is hot, turn one burner off and turn the other(s) to medium. Position the beets over the burner that is off, close the grill's lid, and cook the vegetables for 20 to 40 minutes, depending on their size, turning them occasionally. Beets are done when the tip of a sharp knife easily pierces them.

5. Remove the beets from the grill, skin them, and slice them. Top each portion with the ginger-orange sauce and serve.

Serves 4

•·◆·•

GOOD OLD
CORN-ON-THE-COB

•·◆·•

Grilling corn right in its husks is the easiest way to cook it—and you don't heat up the kitchen with a big pot of boiling water! Always choose the freshest corn possible, with tightly fitting husks and fresh-looking, dry (not soggy) silks.

4 to 8 ears of fresh corn, with husks

1. Preheat the grill for 10 to 15 minutes, with all the burners on high.

2. While the grill is preheating, carefully pull back the husks and remove the silks from each ear. Rinse the corn with cold water, and fold the husks back up around the corn. Tie the tops of the husks together with small pieces of string, or with a husk leaf torn in thin strips.

3. Once the grill is hot, turn one burner off and turn the other(s) to medium. Position the corn over the burner that is off, close the grill's lid, and cook the corn for 25 to 35 minutes, turning it occasionally.

4. Remove the corn from the grill, husk the cobs, and serve hot off the grill.

Serves 4

••◆••
CORN-ON-THE-COB WITH LIME-CHILI BUTTER
••◆••

As good as plain, grilled corn-on-the-cob is, the addition of fresh lime juice and chili powder takes it to another realm.

LIME-CHILI BUTTER
1 tablespoon fresh lime juice
¼ cup butter
1½ teaspoons chili powder
Salt and fresh-ground black pepper to taste

4 ears of fresh corn, with husks

1. Combine the lime-chili butter ingredients in a small saucepan. Cook the mixture over medium heat, stirring occasionally, until the butter is melted. Remove the pan from the heat and reserve at room temperature.

2. Preheat the grill for 10 to 15 minutes, with all the burners on high.

3. While the grill is preheating, husk the corn and remove the silks. Wash the ears in cold water. Tear off squares of aluminum foil large enough to wrap each cob of corn completely. Place one cob of corn on each sheet of foil and brush the ear liberally with the lime-chili butter. Wrap the foil tightly around the corn.

4. Once the grill is hot, turn one burner off and turn the other(s) to medium. Position the corn over the burner that is off, close the grill's lid, and cook the corn for 25 to 35 minutes, turning it occasionally.

5. Remove the corn from the grill, unwrap the ears, pouring any melted butter back over the cobs, and serve hot.

Serves 4

Compound butters, mixtures of butter with herbs, spices, and other flavorings, can transform simple grilled fare into a special meal.

MINTED GRILLED CUCUMBER SPEARS

Grilled cucumber has a pleasant, fresh taste and delicate texture. It goes well with all types of Asian food, and serves as a welcome relief from any type of spicy food, especially when paired with a little fresh mint, as in this recipe.

2 to 3 cucumbers
2 to 3 tablespoons rice wine vinegar
¼ cup chopped fresh mint
Salt to taste

1. Preheat the grill for 10 to 15 minutes, with all the burners on high.

2. While the grill is preheating, peel, seed, and cut the cucumbers lengthwise in quarters.

3. Once the grill is hot, turn all the burners to medium. With the grill's lid open, cook the cucumbers for about 6 minutes, turning them occasionally.

4. Remove the cucumber spears from the grill and arrange them on a serving platter. Splash the cucumbers with the rice wine vinegar, sprinkle with the mint, add salt to taste, and serve warm.

Serves 4

GRILLED EGGPLANT

Eggplant cooked on the grill demands only a light basting of olive oil—a fraction of the amount of oil it takes to sauté eggplant in a pan. As a result, you can taste more of the eggplant's unique flavor—and taste less of the oil. This recipe works with either the long, thin Asian eggplant or the traditional fat, oval ones.

1 large purple eggplant or 3 small Asian eggplant
1 lemon, halved
¼ cup extra-virgin olive oil
1 tablespoon dried thyme leaves, crumbled
Salt and fresh-ground black pepper to taste

1. Peel the eggplant—or leave it unpeeled if you wish. Slice the eggplant in rounds about ⅜ inch thick. Rub the eggplant slices with the lemon. Brush both sides of each eggplant slice with olive oil. Sprinkle each slice with thyme and salt and pepper on both sides.

2. Preheat the grill for 10 to 15 minutes, with all the burners on high.

3. Once the grill is hot, turn all the burners to medium. With the grill's lid open, cook the eggplant slices for about 6 minutes, turning them once. The eggplant will be done when they are well browned and easily pierced with the tip of a sharp knife.

4. Serve the eggplant hot off the grill.

Serves 4

MARINATED EGGPLANT WITH TOMATOES AND FONTINA CHEESE

This is a special vegetable dish, one that some vegetarians might consider a meal in itself! It is superb, however, served as a side dish with grilled chicken or steak—colorful, attractive, and delicious.

2 large eggplant, peeled and sliced ⅜ inch thick
1½ cups homemade or bottled vinaigrette or Italian salad
   dressing
4 to 5 large tomatoes, sliced ⅜ inch thick
¾ pound fontina cheese, sliced ¼ inch thick
Minced fresh basil or parsley

1. Combine the eggplant slices with the vinaigrette in a non-reactive container. Set the eggplant aside to marinate for 30 to 45 minutes.

2. Preheat the grill for 10 to 15 minutes, with all the burners on high.

3. While the grill is preheating, drain the marinade from the container and discard it. Make three-layer stacks with all the eggplant, tomatoes, and cheese: an eggplant slice on the bottom, a tomato slice in the middle, and a cheese slice on top.

4. Once the grill is hot, turn all the burners to medium. Carefully place the stacks of eggplant, tomato, and cheese on the grill, close the grill's lid, and cook the slices for about 8 minutes. The stacks are done when the eggplant is easily pierced with the tip of a sharp knife and the cheese has melted.

5. Serve hot, with a sprinkling of basil or parsley.

Serves 6 to 8 as a side dish

◆◆◆

EGGPLANT, TOMATO, AND PEPPER MÉLANGE

◆◆◆

This dish is as beautiful to look at as it is delicious to eat. It's all about the intense flavors of summer, so it's best to make it when all of the vegetables are at their peak.

1 purple eggplant or 3 small Asian eggplant
4 large tomatoes
3 bell peppers, preferably 1 red, 1 green, and 1 yellow
½ cup extra-virgin olive oil

Salt and fresh-ground black pepper
Chopped fresh basil and parsley

1. Preheat the grill for 10 to 15 minutes, with all the burners on high.

2. While the grill is preheating, peel the eggplant if you wish, and slice it in rounds ⅜ inch to ½ inch thick. Cut the tomatoes in slices and the peppers in rings also about ⅜ inch to ½ inch thick. After slicing, immediately coat the vegetables liberally with some of the olive oil.

3. Once the grill is hot, turn one burner off and turn the other(s) to medium. Position the eggplant, tomato, and pepper slices over the burner that is off, close the grill's lid, and cook for 6 to 10 minutes, turning them once, using a spatula (the tomatoes will not hold together if turned more than once). The eggplant will be done when it is easily pierced with the tip of a sharp knife; the tomatoes simply need to be heated through; and the peppers will be done when they are wilted but still have a little crunch to them.

4. On a large platter, arrange alternating slices of eggplant, tomatoes, and peppers. Drizzle all over with olive oil. Dust the slices liberally with salt and pepper, and sprinkle with basil and parsley. Serve warm, at room temperature, or even cold, the next day.

Serves 6 to 8

••◆••

GRILLED WHOLE
GARLIC BULBS

••◆••

Grilled whole garlic has become increasingly popular, not only for its delicious, slightly nutty flavor, but also for its purported health benefits. Try squeezing the soft cloves of grilled garlic onto slices of crusty Italian bread that has been brushed lightly with olive oil and toasted briefly on the grill. Fantastic!

4 whole garlic bulbs
4 tablespoons extra-virgin olive oil

1. Preheat the grill for 10 to 15 minutes, with all the burners on high.

2. While the grill is preheating, peel away as much of the papery skin from the garlic as possible. Slice off ¼ inch from the top of each bulb. Brush each bulb liberally with olive oil.

3. Once the grill is hot, turn one burner off and turn the other(s) to medium. Position the whole garlic bulbs, cut side down, over the burner that is off, close the grill's lid, and cook for 30 to 40 minutes. The garlic is done when the outside skin has browned and the cloves inside are soft.

4. Remove the garlic bulbs from the grill and let them cool for about 10 minutes, or until cool enough to handle. Squeeze the garlic pulp out of the skins and serve.

Serves 4 to 8

◆◆

GRILLED WHOLE LEEKS

◆◆

Leeks, those underused members of the onion family, are wonderful for grilling. Their strong, earthy flavor mellows on the grill, making leeks a fine mate for any grilled beef. Although a little salt and pepper is all they really need, they also benefit from a sprinkling of balsamic vinegar after grilling.

4 leeks
2 tablespoons extra-virgin olive oil
Salt and fresh-ground black pepper
2 tablespoons balsamic vinegar (optional)

1. Preheat the grill for 10 to 15 minutes, with all the burners on high.

2. While the grill is preheating, cut off most of the green tops from the leeks and split the leeks in half lengthwise. Leave the root ends intact to help keep the leeks from separating on the grill. Wash the leeks well under cold running water and pat them dry. Brush the cut leeks with a little olive oil.

3. Once the grill is hot, turn one burner off and turn the

other(s) to medium. Position the whole leek slices over the burner that is off, close the grill's lid, and cook for 20 to 30 minutes, turning them once. The leeks will be done when they are easily pierced through with the tip of a sharp knife.

4. Remove the leeks from the grill, sprinkle with salt and pepper and balsamic vinegar, if desired, and serve.

Serves 4

A sprinkling of salt, some fresh-ground pepper, and a splash of balsamic vinegar improve the flavor of almost any grilled vegetable.

GRILLED FENNEL WITH ANCHOVY-GARLIC BUTTER

Fennel is served far too infrequently in this country. As a vegetable, it is unique for its combination of crisp texture (somewhat like celery) and mild licorice flavor. This dish is excellent with any grilled fish, and the anchovy-garlic butter makes it particularly good for any Mediterranean-inspired meal.

2 fennel bulbs

ANCHOVY-GARLIC BUTTER
4 tablespoons butter, at room temperature
2 large garlic cloves, pressed
4 anchovy fillets, rinsed
Juice of ½ lemon
1 teaspoon fresh-ground black pepper

1. Trim the ferny tops from the fennel bulbs. Cut the bulb in ½-inch wedges, with the root end left intact so that the fennel will stay together on the grill.

2. Preheat the grill for 10 to 15 minutes, with all the burners on high.

3. While the grill is preheating, make the anchovy-garlic butter. Combine all the ingredients in a bowl. Using a fork, mash the ingredients until the anchovies are in very small bits, and mix well. Keep the butter at room temperature until serving time.

4. Once the grill is hot, turn all the burners to medium. Place the fennel over the heat, close the grill's lid, and cook for 5 to 8 minutes. The fennel is done when it is easily pierced with the tip of a sharp knife.

5. Serve hot off the grill, with the anchovy-garlic butter spread on top of each slice.

Serves 4

GRILLED MARINATED MUSHROOMS

Although this recipe was originally developed for standard-issue white or brown mushrooms, it works equally well for any of the exotic mushrooms that are becoming available in more and more markets across the country. Common white or brown mushrooms have one advantage, however: they are very easy to grill because they are easy to thread on skewers. Some of the more delicate, exotic mushrooms are more difficult to handle on the grill—more difficult, but worth the effort nonetheless.

MARINADE
½ cup dry red wine
¼ cup olive oil
Juice of ½ lemon
1 large garlic clove, pressed
2 teaspoons dried thyme leaves, crumbled
1 teaspoon salt
½ teaspoon fresh-cracked peppercorns

1 pound whole mushrooms, washed and stems trimmed
12 bamboo skewers, soaked in water

1. In a large, nonreactive container, combine all the marinade ingredients and mix well. Toss the mushrooms in the marinade. Cover the container and refrigerate for 1 to 2 hours, stirring the mushrooms occasionally.

The simplicity of the grilling process demands high-quality raw ingredients, even more so than other, more complicated cooking methods. When you grill, always start with the freshest and best ingredients.

2. Preheat the grill for 10 to 15 minutes, with all the burners on high.

3. While the grill is preheating, drain the marinade from the container and discard it. Thread the mushrooms onto the skewers.

4. Once the grill is hot, turn one burner off and turn the other(s) to medium. Place the skewered mushrooms over the burner that is off, close the grill's lid, and cook until the mushrooms are tender, about 8 to 12 minutes, depending on the size of the mushrooms. Turn the mushrooms once during cooking.

5. Serve the mushrooms hot off the grill. Alternatively, let them cool to room temperature, slice them if you wish, and serve as an appetizer on pieces of crunchy, toasted bread.

Serves 3 to 4

PORTOBELLO MUSHROOM BURGERS

With the rise of vegetarianism in this country comes a rise in the number of new recipes for non–meat eaters. Certainly one of the best is the portobello mushroom burger, which even some carnivores like better than the original "quarter-pound" version.

4 large whole portobello mushrooms
1 lemon, halved
2 tablespoons extra-virgin olive oil
Dried thyme leaves, crumbled
Salt and fresh-ground black pepper

2 tablespoons butter, at room temperature
4 good-quality hamburger buns
Arugula, watercress, or lettuce leaves
Tomato slices
Onion slices
Condiments of your choice, such as Dijon mustard, mayonnaise, or ketchup

1. Preheat the grill for 10 to 15 minutes, with all the burners on high.

2. While the grill is preheating, rub the portobello mushrooms with a soft, damp cloth to clean them. Then rub the mushrooms with the lemon halves. Brush the mushrooms lightly with olive oil and sprinkle with thyme, salt, and pepper. Spread the softened butter on the face of each hamburger bun half.

3. Once the grill is hot, turn one burner off and turn the other(s) to medium. Position the mushrooms over the burner that is off, close the grill's lid, and cook the mushrooms for 8 to 10 minutes, turning them once. A mushroom is done when it is easily pierced with the tip of a sharp knife. Meanwhile, toast the hamburger buns on the grill for about 2 minutes per side.

4. Place the mushrooms on the buns and serve. Let the guests add the toppings and condiments as they prefer.

Serves 4

⋄◆⋄

WHITE ONION KEBOBS WITH ROSEMARY AND BALSAMIC VINEGAR

⋄◆⋄

Small white boiling onions are great candidates for grilling: they thread easily on skewers, they cook relatively quickly, and best of all, they have an intense onion flavor that goes well with almost any grilled meat.

16 to 24 small white boiling onions
12 bamboo skewers, soaked in water
4 tablespoons extra-virgin olive oil
1 tablespoon crumbled fresh rosemary leaves
Salt and fresh-ground black pepper
2 tablespoons balsamic vinegar (optional)

1. Preheat the grill for 10 to 15 minutes, with all the burners on high.

2. While the grill is preheating, carefully peel the skins from the onions. Thread the onions onto two parallel skewers, with the onions' sides touching. Combine the olive oil and rosemary in a bowl and brush the mixture onto the onions.

3. Once the grill is hot, turn one burner off and turn the other(s) to medium. Position the skewered onions over the burner that is off, close the grill's lid, and cook the onions for 15 to 20 minutes, turning them occasionally. The onions will be done when they are lightly browned and are easily pierced through with the tip of a sharp knife.

4. Remove the onions from the grill, sprinkle them with salt and pepper, add a dash of balsamic vinegar, if desired, and serve.

Serves 4

⋄⋆◆⋆⋄

ORIENTAL GRILLED GREEN ONIONS

⋄⋆◆⋆⋄

Not many people think of grilling green onions (or scallions), but they make an unusual and tasty side dish for grilled beef or lamb, and are particularly good with any Asian-inspired recipe.

> *12 green onions, root ends and green tops trimmed*
>   *slightly*
> *2 tablespoons sesame oil*
> *1 tablespoon soy sauce*
> *1 teaspoon hoisin sauce*

1. Preheat the grill for 10 to 15 minutes, with all the burners on high.

2. While the grill is preheating, combine the sesame oil, soy sauce, and hoisin sauce in a bowl and brush the mixture on the green onions.

3. Once the grill is hot, turn all the burners to medium. Position the green onions perpendicular to the grill bars. With the lid open, grill the green onions for 3 to 4 minutes, turning them once. The onions will be done when they are lightly browned.

4. Serve the onions hot off the grill.

Serves 4

GRILLED ONION SLICES

These onion slices not only are delicious on hamburgers, but they also make a flavorful side dish to any grilled meat. Brown-skinned onions have the most intense flavor, sweetened somewhat by grilling, but both the milder, white-skinned onions and red onions can be grilled successfully as well.

2 to 4 onions, peeled and sliced ⅜ inch thick
4 tablespoons extra-virgin olive oil
1 tablespoon dried rosemary or thyme leaves, crumbled
Salt and fresh-ground black pepper

1. Preheat the grill for 10 to 15 minutes, with all the burners on high.

2. While the grill is preheating, combine the olive oil with the rosemary or thyme in a bowl and brush the mixture onto the onions.

3. Once the grill is hot, turn all the burners to medium. Place the onion slices over the heat, close the grill's lid, and cook them for about 2 to 4 minutes, turning them once (using a spatula). The onions will be done when they are lightly browned.

4. Remove the onions from the grill, sprinkle them with salt and pepper, and serve hot.

Serves 4

GRILLED PEPPERS

Any pepper, mild or hot, can be grilled. Although grilling makes peppers less pungent, it does not make hot varieties any less hot. Grilled peppers go with virtually any grilled food, and are flavorful enough on their own not to require any adornment, except for salt and pepper. *Note:* You can prepare these peppers for a handful or a houseful: the sheer quantity doesn't matter, as long as you make enough to satisfy everyone.

Whole fresh peppers, any variety
Olive oil
Salt and fresh-ground black pepper

1. Preheat the grill for 10 to 15 minutes, with all the burners on high.

2. While the grill is preheating, wash the peppers under cold water, dry them, and rub them with a little olive oil.

3. Once the grill is hot, turn one burner off and turn the other(s) to medium. Position the peppers over the burner that is off, close the grill's lid, and cook the peppers for 10 to 20 minutes, turning them occasionally. The peppers will be done when they are lightly browned and collapse on themselves.

4. Remove the peppers from the grill, and stem and seed each one. Serve hot off the grill, sprinkled with salt and pepper to taste.

MARINATED ROASTED PEPPERS

The gas grill is tops when it comes to roasting peppers quickly and easily. Take the peppers one step further by marinating them and they make a fantastic addition to any pasta dish. They also hold their own as an appetizer when teamed up with some crusty Italian or French bread and a soft cheese, such as Teleme or fresh mozzarella. For a visual, as well as gustatory, treat, roast peppers of all colors: green, red, yellow, and orange.

Unlike grilling most other foods, the point of grilling peppers is to actually char the skin (but not the flesh). The length of time it takes to do so depends on the size and thickness of the peppers' walls. You'll need to keep your eye on the peppers while they roast, turning them frequently as the skin on one side or another becomes charred. The more evenly charred the skins are, the easier it will be to remove them.

4 fresh bell peppers, preferably an assortment of colors
4 tablespoons olive oil
2 tablespoons red wine vinegar
Salt and fresh-ground black pepper to taste

1. Preheat the grill for 10 to 15 minutes, with all the burners on high.

2. Once the grill is hot, place the peppers directly over the heat (with all the burners still on high), leaving the grill's lid open, and cook them for 10 to 15 minutes, or until the skins are blackened all over and the peppers have collapsed on themselves, or even split. Keep your eye on the peppers while they roast, turning them frequently as the skin on one side or another becomes charred.

3. Transfer the peppers to a brown paper bag or bowl, seal it tightly, and let them "sweat" until soft, 15 minutes or so.

4. Once the peppers have cooled, use a small, sharp knife to remove the stems and skins, and to scrape away the seeds and membrane inside the peppers—a messy proposition, but definitely worth it. Do not wash the peeled peppers, because that will greatly diminish their natural flavor.

5. Cut the roasted peppers in thin strips and place them in a nonreactive bowl. Add the oil, vinegar, and salt and pepper. Set the peppers aside for at least 30 minutes at room temperature, or refrigerate them in an airtight container for several days.

6. Serve the peppers warm or at room temperature.

Serves 4 to 8

◆

GRILLED CHEESE-STUFFED PEPPERS
◆

This recipe is a grilled version of the popular Mexican specialty chiles rellenos. They are wonderful as an appetizer or as a side dish for grilled beef or chicken.

4 large green chiles (preferably the dark green chile
poblano or chile pasilla; otherwise, the long green
Anaheim variety)

3 whole medium tomatoes
¼ teaspoon ground cumin
¼ teaspoon dried oregano leaves, crumbled
Salt and fresh-ground black pepper to taste
1 cup coarse-grated Monterey jack cheese
Vegetable oil

1. Preheat the grill for 10 to 15 minutes, with all the burners on high.

2. While the grill is preheating, wash and dry the peppers.

3. Once the grill is hot, place the chiles directly over the heat (with all the burners still on high), leaving the grill's lid open, and cook them for 10 to 15 minutes, or until the skins are blackened all over and the peppers have collapsed on themselves, or even split. Keep your eye on the peppers while they roast, turning them frequently as the skin on one side or another becomes charred.

4. Transfer the chiles to a brown paper bag or bowl, seal it tightly, and let them "sweat" until soft, 15 minutes or so.

5. After the peppers have been removed from the grill, turn one burner off and turn the other(s) to medium. Position the tomatoes over the burner that is off, close the grill's lid, and cook them for about 15 minutes. Do not turn the tomatoes.

6. Transfer the tomatoes to a small dish and chop them roughly (skins and all). Add the cumin and oregano, and season to taste with salt and pepper.

7. When the peppers are cool enough to handle, peel away the charred outer skin. Make a lengthwise cut in each pepper, leaving the stem end attached, and remove the seeds and as much of the veins as possible. Stuff each pepper gently with cheese, fold the cut ends together, and seal up the cut with a toothpick or two.

8. Oil the stuffed peppers lightly and place them over the burner that is off. Close the grill's lid and cook just until the cheese is melted, about 8 minutes.

9. Serve the peppers with the chopped seasoned tomatoes as a sauce.

Serves 4 as a side dish, 2 as a main dish

Using a simple trigger-pump spray bottle filled with olive oil is a fast and easy way to apply a thin coating of oil to any food before grilling.

·◆·

"BAKED" POTATOES ON THE GRILL

·◆·

If you're planning to serve baked potatoes as a side dish for a grilled entree, you might as well "bake" the potatoes on the grill, too. It saves time and energy, and avoids heating up the kitchen.

> 4 Idaho or russet baking potatoes
> Butter, sour cream, and chopped fresh chives, for toppings
>   (optional)
> Salt and fresh-ground black pepper to taste

1. Preheat the grill for 10 to 15 minutes, with all the burners on high.

2. While the grill is preheating, scrub the potatoes well under running water and poke a few incisions into each one with the tip of a sharp knife. Wrap each potato in two layers of aluminum foil.

3. Once the grill is hot, turn one burner off and turn the other(s) to medium. Position the potatoes over the burner that is off, close the grill's lid, and cook the potatoes for 45 to 60 minutes. The potatoes will be done when they are pierced easily with the tip of a sharp knife. If you prefer crisp skins, remove the aluminum foil for the last 10 minutes or so of the cooking time.

4. Serve the potatoes hot off the grill with plenty of butter, sour cream, chives, and salt and pepper.

Serves 4

·◆·

GRILLED POTATO SKINS

·◆·

This recipe is dedicated to those who say that the best part of a baked potato is the skin. Grilled potato skins have an extra crispiness that many people find irresistible.

> 4 Idaho or russet baking potatoes
> 4 teaspoons butter, melted

As tempting as it may be to cook foods directly over the hot burners, most of the time you'll have greater success if you turn one burner off and cook the food indirectly over the burner that is off, with the grill's lid down. Although indirect cooking takes a little longer, it virtually guarantees that you won't ever burn grilled food again.

*Butter, sour cream, and chopped fresh chives, for toppings
   (optional)*
Salt and fresh-ground black pepper to taste

1. Scrub the potatoes well under cold water, and using the tip of a sharp knife, poke a few steam vents in each potato. Bake the potatoes in a preheated 350° F oven for 60 minutes. Remove the potatoes from the oven and let them cool. Cut a slit in each baked potato and remove all but ¼ inch or so of the flesh. Flatten each potato with the heel of your hand. Lightly brush the insides of the potatoes with butter.

2. Preheat the grill for 10 to 15 minutes, with all the burners on high.

3. Once the grill is hot, turn all the burners to medium. Grill the potato skins for about 10 minutes, with the grill's lid open, turning them once.

4. Serve the skins hot off the grill with plenty of butter, sour cream, chives, and salt and pepper.

Serves 4

SKEWERED HERBED POTATOES

Roasted new potatoes, seasoned liberally with fresh herbs and doused with garlic, are hard to resist. This classic flavor combination is well suited to grilled fish or poultry. Remember, threading new potatoes on bamboo skewers makes them much easier to manage than individual ones, loose on the grill.

20 new potatoes, each about the size of a golf ball
⅓ cup olive oil
*3 tablespoons chopped fresh herbs (dill, basil, oregano,
   thyme, rosemary, mint, or any combination)*
2 garlic cloves, pressed
1 teaspoon fresh-ground black pepper
Salt to taste
6 bamboo skewers, soaked in water

1. Preheat the grill for 10 to 15 minutes, with all the burners on high.

2. While the grill is preheating, wash and scrub the new potatoes in cold water. Pat them dry, but do not peel them. Place the potatoes in a bowl and toss them with the oil, herbs, garlic, pepper, and salt. Thread 5 potatoes, with their sides touching, on each skewer.

3. Once the grill is hot, turn one burner off and turn the other(s) to medium. Place the potato skewers over the burner that is off, close the grill's lid, and cook the potatoes for about 30 minutes, turning them every 10 minutes or so. The potatoes will be done when they are easily pierced with the tip of a sharp knife.

4. Serve the potatoes hot off the grill.

Serves 4

·•◆•·
ROSEMARY POTATO WEDGES
·•◆•·

Brown-skinned baking potatoes, quartered lengthwise in long wedges and cooked on the grill, are like big, crisp french fries, but without all the oil. The addition of a little rosemary makes them the perfect accompaniment for any cut of beef or any type of poultry. If desired, sprinkle a little coarse salt on the potato wedges after grilling—it really sparks the flavors into life.

> *4 large Idaho or russet baking potatoes*
> *⅓ cup extra-virgin olive oil*
> *1 tablespoon crushed dried rosemary*
> *Fresh-ground black pepper to taste*
> *Coarse or regular table salt to taste*

1. Preheat the grill for 10 to 15 minutes, with all the burners on high.

2. While the grill is preheating, wash and scrub the potatoes under cold water. Pat them dry with paper towels, but do not peel them. Cut the potatoes lengthwise in wedges and place them in a bowl. Toss the potatoes with the oil, rosemary, and pepper.

3. Once the grill is hot, turn one burner off and turn the other(s) to medium. Place the potato wedges over the burner that is off, close the grill's lid, and cook the potatoes for 30 to 40 minutes, turning them every 10 minutes or so. The potatoes will be done when they are easily pierced with the tip of a sharp knife.

4. Serve the potatoes hot off the grill, sprinkled with a little coarse salt, if desired.

Serves 4

⋄⋆◆⋆⋄

ROAST SWEET POTATOES WITH CILANTRO-LIME BUTTER

⋄⋆◆⋆⋄

This perfect combination of Southern Hemisphere flavors is guaranteed to turn any sweet potato hater into a sweet potato lover.

4 sweet potatoes
¼ cup butter, softened
2 tablespoons fresh lime juice
2 tablespoons chopped fresh cilantro

1. Preheat the grill for 10 to 15 minutes, with all the burners on high.

2. Scrub the sweet potatoes under running water and poke a few incisions into each with the tip of a sharp knife. Wrap each sweet potato in two layers of aluminum foil.

3. Once the grill is hot, turn one burner off and turn the other(s) to medium. Position the potatoes over the burner that is off, close the grill's lid, and cook the potatoes for about 60 minutes, turning and rotating them once or twice. The sweet potatoes will be done when they are pierced easily, all the way through, with the tip of a sharp knife. If you prefer crisp skins, remove the aluminum foil for the last 10 minutes or so of the cooking time.

4. While the potatoes roast, combine the butter, lime juice, and chopped cilantro. Set aside at room temperature.

5. To serve, remove the potatoes from the foil. Split each one open and top with the flavored butter. Serve hot.

Serves 4

◆

GRILLED SUMMER SQUASH

◆

All types of summer squash—zucchini, yellow crooknecks, pattypans, you name it—can be grilled easily. Although convention has dictated that squash be cut in pieces and threaded onto skewers for grilling, it's actually preferable to cook them whole and slice them later. Both the flavor and texture of any summer squash are enhanced with this method.

> *4 small summer squash, about 1½ to 2 pounds*
> *4 tablespoons olive oil*
> *Chopped fresh parsley*
> *Salt and fresh-ground black pepper to taste*

1. Preheat the grill for 10 to 15 minutes, with all the burners on high.

2. Wash the squash in cold water and pat them dry. Trim the tops and bottoms of the squash, and then rub the olive oil all over them.

3. Once the grill is hot, turn one burner off and turn the other(s) to medium. Position the whole squash over the burner that is off, close the grill's lid, and cook the squash for about 12 to 20 minutes (depending on the size and variety of the squash), turning the squash as needed. The squash will be done when they are easily pierced with the tip of a sharp knife.

4. Transfer the squash to a cutting board, slice them, toss them with parsley and salt and pepper, and serve.

Serves 4

◆◆◆

HONEY-GLAZED WINTER SQUASH EN BROCHETTE

◆◆◆

When cut in cubes of a manageable size (1 to 1½ inches), winter squash grills up beautifully. Naturally sweet winter squash pairs well with grilled ham and pork recipes.

1½ pounds winter squash, peeled, seeded, and cut in
*   1-inch to 1½-inch cubes*
6 bamboo skewers, soaked in water
½ cup butter, melted
2 tablespoons honey or pure maple syrup

1. Preheat the grill for 10 to 15 minutes, with all the burners on high.

2. While the grill is preheating, thread the squash cubes onto the skewers, with the cubes' sides touching. Brush the squash liberally with some of the melted butter.

3. Once the grill is hot, turn one burner off and turn the other(s) to medium. Position the skewered squash over the burner that is off, close the grill's lid, and cook the squash for 15 to 20 minutes, turning the skewers once. The squash will be done when it is easily pierced with the tip of a sharp knife.

4. In a bowl, combine the remaining melted butter with the honey or maple syrup.

5. Transfer the squash to your work surface, remove the skewers, and toss the cubes lightly with the sweetened butter. Serve hot.

Serves 4

SKEWERED PLUM TOMATOES WITH GARLIC AND BASIL

These meaty, oval-shaped paste tomatoes (most often the Roma variety, or one of its offspring) are great for grilling. Although they can be grilled whole, they are more attractive on the plate if they are cut in half lengthwise. To hold them securely while they cook, thread them onto two parallel bamboo skewers.

8 plum tomatoes, halved lengthwise
12 bamboo skewers, soaked in water
¼ cup extra-virgin olive oil
2 garlic cloves, minced
¼ cup minced fresh basil
Salt and fresh-ground black pepper to taste

1. Preheat the grill for 10 to 15 minutes, with all the burners on high.

2. While the grill is preheating, thread the tomato halves, cut side up, onto 2 parallel skewers. Rub the olive oil on all sides.

3. Once the grill is hot, turn one burner off and turn the other(s) to medium. Position the skewered tomatoes over the burner that is off, close the grill's lid, and cook for 8 to 10 minutes, turning them once. The tomatoes will be done when they are heated through and soft to the touch.

4. Remove the tomatoes from the grill, sprinkle them with garlic and basil, season with salt and pepper, and serve.

Serves 4

GARLICKY GRILLED TOMATOES

These tomatoes are delicious as an accompaniment to virtually any grilled meat. They can also serve as the base for a very easy and tasty pasta sauce. To make the sauce, peel the cooked tomatoes if you wish, mince them, and place them in a bowl. Add a couple of tablespoons of olive oil, salt, fresh-ground black pepper, and chopped herbs if desired. Mix everything well and serve on top of spaghetti for a delightful, fresh-tasting summer pasta.

4 medium to large tomatoes
4 garlic cloves, pressed
4 teaspoons extra-virgin olive oil
Salt and fresh-ground black pepper
2 to 4 tablespoons minced fresh oregano, basil, or both

1. Preheat the grill for 10 to 15 minutes, with all the burners on high.

2. While the grill is preheating, cut off the top ⅜ inch of each tomato. If you have a tomato corer, use it to remove about half of the core; otherwise use the tip of a very sharp paring knife. Press 1 clove of garlic into the core cavity of each tomato. Drizzle about 1 teaspoon of olive oil over the top of each tomato, and dust with salt and pepper.

3. Once the grill is hot, turn one burner off and turn the other(s) to medium. Position the tomatoes, cut side up, over the burner that is off. Close the grill's lid and cook the tomatoes for 10 to 15 minutes, depending on their size and degree of ripeness. Do not turn the tomatoes. They will be done when they are heated through and soft to the touch.

4. Using a spatula, carefully transfer the tomatoes to a serving platter; they do tend to split easily at this point. Sprinkle the tomatoes liberally with oregano or basil, or both, and serve hot.

Serves 4

GRILLED WHOLE PESTO TOMATOES

Basil-rich pesto and red-ripe tomatoes are natural partners, made even more intensely delicious by grilling. As simple as this side dish is, it is one of the best.

PESTO
2 garlic cloves
¼ teaspoon salt
1 tablespoon pine nuts, toasted
2 tablespoons extra-virgin olive oil
3 tablespoons butter, softened
20 large fresh basil leaves
Fresh-ground black pepper

4 medium to large tomatoes
2 teaspoons extra-virgin olive oil
Salt and fresh-ground black pepper

1. To make the pesto, combine the garlic, salt, pine nuts, olive oil, and butter in a food processor and process until smooth. Add the basil and continue to process until well mixed. Season the pesto to taste with pepper, and set aside.

2. Preheat the grill for 10 to 15 minutes, with all the burners on high.

3. While the grill is preheating, cut off the top ⅜ inch of each tomato. If you have a tomato corer, use it to remove about half of the core; otherwise use the tip of a very sharp paring knife. Fill the cavity of each tomato with the pesto, drizzle about ½ teaspoon of the olive oil over the top, and dust with salt and pepper.

4. Once the grill is hot, turn one burner off and turn the other(s) to medium. Position the tomatoes, cut side up, over the burner that is off. Close the grill's lid and cook the tomatoes for 10 to 15 minutes, depending on their size and degree of ripeness. Do not turn the tomatoes. They will be done when they are heated through and soft to the touch.

5. Using a spatula, carefully transfer the tomatoes to a serving platter; they do tend to split easily at this point. Serve at once.

Serves 4

To dramatically enhance the flavor and texture of a less-than-perfect or out-of-season tomato, just grill it!

CHERRY TOMATOES
EN BROCHETTE

Cherry tomatoes are often surprisingly flavorful for their size and, fortunately, are available in a nicely ripened state year-round. Threaded onto skewers, cherry tomatoes are the essence of simplicity to grill.

24 cherry tomatoes
12 bamboo skewers, soaked in water
¼ cup olive oil
2 garlic cloves, pressed
Salt and fresh-ground black pepper

1. Preheat the grill for 10 to 15 minutes, with all the burners on high.

2. While the grill is preheating, thread the tomatoes onto two parallel skewers. Combine the olive oil and garlic in a bowl and brush the mixture onto the tomatoes.

3. Once the grill is hot, turn one burner off and turn the other(s) to medium. Position the skewered cherry tomatoes over the burner that is off, close the grill's lid, and cook for 8 to 10 minutes. The tomatoes will be done when they are heated through and soft to the touch.

4. Remove the tomatoes from the grill, sprinkle them with salt and pepper, and serve.

Serves 4

TOMATOES STUFFED WITH DUCHESS POTATOES

·•◆•·

This combination of tomatoes and potatoes is not only unusual, but also beautiful—and delicious.

DUCHESS POTATOES
6 large baking potatoes, scrubbed and peeled
¼ cup milk
4 to 6 tablespoons butter
Salt and fresh-ground black pepper to taste
2 eggs, beaten

8 large tomatoes
1 cup grated Swiss cheese
Chopped fresh parsley, for garnish

1. To make the duchess potatoes, boil the potatoes in plenty of salted water until very tender and easily pierced with the tip of a sharp knife, from 15 to 30 minutes. Drain the potatoes well and return them to the pot. Mash the potatoes, adding the milk and butter, until they have reached a fairly smooth consistency. Season with salt and pepper to taste. Beat in the eggs and set the potatoes aside briefly to cool.

2. Slice off the top ½ inch of each tomato. Using a sharp-edged spoon (a melon-baller or serrated grapefruit spoon works well), hollow out the tomatoes by removing the meat, being careful not to pierce the skin. Set the tomatoes aside.

3. Spoon the slightly cooled potatoes into a plastic bag and force them into one of the bag's bottom corners (as in a pastry bag). With a pair of scissors, cut the tip off that corner to create an opening about ¾ inch wide. Squeeze the duchess potatoes out of the bag and into each hollowed-out tomato, mounding the potatoes slightly on top. Press a tablespoon or so of the grated Swiss cheese on top of the potatoes in each tomato.

4. Preheat the grill for 10 to 15 minutes, with all the burners on high.

5. Once the grill is hot, turn one burner off and turn the other(s) to medium. Position the stuffed tomatoes over the burner that is off, close the grill's lid, and cook for 15 to 20 minutes. They will be done when the duchess potatoes are heated through and the cheese has melted.

6. Using a spatula, carefully transfer the tomatoes to a serving platter; they do tend to split easily at this point. Sprinkle parsley over the tomatoes and serve hot.

Serves 8

GRILLED MARINATED TOFU

These days, mixed households of carnivores and vegetarians are not at all unusual. If you invite a group over to your house for a cookout, some of the guests will almost certainly be vegetarians. When you're planning a grilled meal featuring a meat dish, you can avoid a problem by having some tofu on hand (the hard, or firm, variety). Simply marinate the tofu and then grill it alongside the rest of the meal for a delicious entrée.

> *1-pound block hard (sometimes called firm) tofu*
> *1 cup bottled teriyaki sauce*
> *¼ cup vegetable or sesame oil*

1. Preheat the grill for 10 to 15 minutes, with all the burners on high.

2. While the grill is preheating, slice the tofu ½ inch thick and put the slices in a shallow dish. Combine the teriyaki sauce and oil in a bowl and pour the marinade over the tofu. Let the tofu stand at room temperature until grilling time.

3. Once the grill is hot, turn one burner off and turn the other(s) to medium. Place the tofu over the burner that is off, close the grill's lid, and cook the slices for 8 to 10 minutes, turning them once (using a spatula). The tofu will be done when it is heated through and lightly "toasted" on the outside.

4. Serve immediately.

Serves 2 to 3

Wood smoke may overpower the flavor of most vegetables, but a perforated foil packet of herbs, such as oregano or rosemary, in the grill will add a delicate flavor.

⁺⁺◆⁺⁺
TOFU KEBOBS
⁺⁺◆⁺⁺

Combining meat and vegetables on the same skewer has always caused problems for grillers, simply because the meat usually takes much longer than the vegetables to cook. When it comes to tofu, however, that problem is solved, because tofu and vegetables cook at about the same rate. Marinating all the ingredients in a little teriyaki sauce greatly enhances their flavor.

1-pound block hard (sometimes called firm) tofu, cut in
  1¼-inch cubes
12 cherry tomatoes
2 bell peppers (any color), cut in 1¼-inch squares
12 white mushrooms, rinsed and stems trimmed
12 bamboo skewers, soaked in water
1½ cups bottled teriyaki sauce
⅓ cup vegetable or sesame oil

1. Preheat the grill for 10 to 15 minutes, with all the burners on high.

2. While the grill is preheating, thread the tofu cubes, cherry tomatoes, bell peppers, and mushrooms in turn onto the skewers. Place the skewered vegetables in a shallow container. Combine the teriyaki sauce and oil in a bowl, and pour the marinade over the skewers. Let the vegetables stand at room temperature until grilling time.

3. Once the grill is hot, turn one burner off and turn the other(s) to medium. Place the skewers over the burner that is off, close the grill's lid, and cook the vegetables for 8 to 10 minutes, turning them once (using a spatula). The skewers will be done when the tofu is heated through and lightly "toasted" on the outside and the vegetables are just beginning to soften.

4. Serve immediately.

Serves 4

✦✦◆✦✦

MIXED VEGETABLE BROCHETTES

✦✦◆✦✦

When you try to combine meat and vegetables on one skewer, one or the other usually turns out imperfect. It is far better to separate the meat from the vegetables on different skewers. That said, it's certainly okay to combine a variety of vegetables on one skewer—the brochettes will be attractive, and all the vegetables will be cooked "just right." The types of vegetables listed here should be considered suggestions only— and you decide how much of each to cook, enough to make 12 skewers.

Red, green, or yellow bell peppers, seeded, deveined, and
  cut in 1-inch squares
Whole button mushrooms, scrubbed well and stems
  trimmed
Onions, peeled and cut in 1-inch cubes
Zucchini or other summer squash, cut in 1-inch slices
Cherry or yellow pear tomatoes
Eggplant, peeled and cut in 1-inch cubes
12 bamboo skewers, soaked in water
Olive oil
Salt and fresh-ground black pepper
Dried thyme leaves

1. Preheat the grill for 10 to 15 minutes, with all the burners on high.

2. While the grill is preheating, thread the vegetables in an alternating pattern onto the skewers. Pierce the mushrooms sideways through the cap, and spear the zucchini through the skin, so that the cut sides face toward the grill. Coat all the vegetables with a liberal amount of olive oil, salt and pepper, and a sprinkling of thyme.

3. Once the grill is hot, turn all the burners to medium. Place the brochettes directly over the heat, close the grill's lid, and cook the vegetables for about 10 minutes, turning them occasionally. The eggplant will be done when it is easily pierced with the tip of a sharp knife; the tomatoes simply need to be heated through; and the peppers will be ready when they are wilted but still a little crunchy.

4. Serve the vegetables hot off the grill.

Serves 4 to 6

••◆••

GRILLED RATATOUILLE

••◆••

The grilled version of ratatouille—a classic vegetable mixture from the Provence region of France—is actually far more authentic than the more common stovetop version. Not long ago, all ratatouille was cooked over an open grill; indeed, many traditional chefs throughout France still cook the vegetables over the coals. This dish actually tastes better the day after it has been assembled, so you might want to plan ahead.

1 large eggplant, peeled and cut in 1-inch cubes
1 medium onion, cut in quarters
3 zucchini (or any other summer squash), cut in ½-inch
  rounds
2 bell peppers, cut in strips about 1 inch wide
12 paste or plum tomatoes (or 18 cherry tomatoes)
12 to 24 bamboo skewers, soaked in water
½ cup extra-virgin olive oil
3 to 4 garlic cloves, minced
½ teaspoon dried oregano
1 to 2 tablespoons chopped fresh basil
Fresh lemon juice or balsamic vinegar to taste
Salt and fresh-ground black pepper to taste

1. Thread the eggplant, onion, zucchini, bell peppers, and tomatoes on separate skewers. Keep all of each type of vegetable on separate skewers, and use 2 parallel skewers as needed. Brush the brochettes liberally with some of the olive oil.

2. Preheat the grill for 10 to 15 minutes, with all the burners on high.

3. Once the grill is hot, turn one burner off and turn the other(s) to medium. Position the skewered vegetables over the burner that is turned off, close the grill's lid, and cook for 15 to 25 minutes, turning the brochettes as needed. Some vegetables, such as the tomatoes, will cook more quickly than the others. With the exception of the onions, which should be thoroughly wilted when done, remove each type of vegetable while it still has a little crunch left.

4. As each type of vegetable is done, slide the pieces off the skewers into a large bowl. Halve or quarter the tomatoes before mixing them with the other vegetables. Season the mixture with olive oil, garlic, oregano, and basil. Taste the vegetables and add lemon juice or balsamic vinegar and salt and pepper to taste. Toss the mixture lightly.

5. Serve the ratatouille immediately, or cover the bowl and refrigerate it until the next day.

Serves 6 to 8

◆

FRUITS AND DESSERTS

◆

CHAPTER EIGHT
FRUITS AND DESSERTS

·◆·

If most home cooks think grilling vegetables is some-what unusual, grilling fruits and other sweet or dessert foods may seem downright strange. Be advised, however, that grilling fruit makes good culinary sense, especially because there's something about the grilling process that transforms even slightly inferior, underripe fruit into a first-rate dish.

Some fruits, such as apples and pineapples, can be used as either a dessert or a side dish, especially when paired with smoked or cured ham. The natural sweetness of the fruit complements the saltiness of the ham perfectly.

Fruits can also be grilled in foil packets, while you eat your main dish. Simply place the fruit on a sheet of heavy-duty aluminum foil, and drizzle melted butter and a little lemon juice over it. If you like, add a little sweetener or fruit liqueur, and perhaps a sprinkling of cinnamon. Bring the edges of the package together and fold them over to seal the foil. Put the foil packet on a warming rack or over a preheated burner that has been turned off. By the time you are ready for dessert, the fruit should be heated through. Use the grilled fruit as a topping for toasted pound cake, angel food cake, biscuits, or ice cream.

If you're up for something unusual and impressive, be sure to try the Dessert Bruschetta with Cheese and Honey. As unlikely as it sounds, the flavors are extraordinary.

CARAMELIZED FRUIT KEBOBS

When I was experimenting with grilled fruit, this recipe came as both a surprise and a delight. Apples, peaches, and plums work best; the peaches and plums need not even be fully ripe to turn out delicious. These fruits are wonderful warm off the grill—kind of like a pie without the crust.

> The delicate flavor of fruit can be overwhelmed by smoke. Save your wood chips for heartier foods, such as beef, chicken, or pork.

2 apples
3 or 4 plums
2 or 3 peaches
4 or more tablespoons butter, melted
4 or more tablespoons granulated sugar
12 bamboo skewers, soaked in water

1. Preheat the grill for 10 to 15 minutes, with all the burners on high.

2. While the grill is preheating, cut all the fruit into 1-inch to 1½-inch chunks (rather than wedges). Combine the butter and sugar in a bowl and mix well. Thread the fruit chunks in turn onto the skewers, and then brush them liberally with the sugared butter.

3. Once the grill is hot, turn one burner off and turn the other(s) to medium. Position the skewered fruit over the burner that is off, close the grill's lid, and cook the fruit skewers for 6 to 10 minutes, turning them occasionally.

4. Serve the fruit warm off the grill.

Serves 4

GRILLED APPLE SLICES

Grilled apple slices are a wonderful accompaniment to all kinds of grilled pork dishes. Choose a cooking apple such as Rome Beauty or Granny Smith for the best texture and taste. A splash of balsamic vinegar on top of the grilled apples really enhances their flavor.

4 apples
¼ to ½ cup melted butter
2 tablespoons balsamic vinegar (optional)

1. Preheat the grill for 10 to 15 minutes, with all the burners on high.

2. While the grill is preheating, peel the apples, if desired. Use an apple corer to remove the cores and seeds. Then slice the apples into rounds ½ inch thick. Coat the apple slices liberally with the butter.

3. Once the grill is hot, turn one burner off and turn the other(s) to medium. Position the apples over the burner that is off, close the grill's lid, and cook the fruit for 5 to 8 minutes, turning the slices occasionally.

4. Serve the apples in bowls, warm off the grill, splashed with a little balsamic vinegar, if desired.

Serves 4

⁺⁺◆⁺⁺

GRILLED BANANAS

⁺⁺◆⁺⁺

Grilling softens bananas and intensifies their flavor. They are an incredible treat hot off the grill, combined with vanilla ice cream and a little chocolate sauce. Heavenly!

4 bananas, just ripe, halved lengthwise, with skins intact

1. Preheat the grill for 10 to 15 minutes, with all the burners on high.

2. Once the grill is hot, turn one burner off and turn the other(s) to medium. Position the bananas, skin side down, over the burner that is off, close the grill's lid and cook the bananas for 5 to 8 minutes. Turn the bananas cut side down and grill them for an additional 2 minutes.

3. Serve the bananas hot off the grill.

Serves 4

TROPICAL GRILLED BANANAS

This great flavor combination is excellent with vanilla ice cream. These bananas also make a great topping for Toasted Pound Cake (page 214).

3 tablespoons butter
⅓ cup packed brown sugar
Juice of 2 limes
4 bananas, firm but ripe, halved lengthwise, with skins
    intact

1. Preheat the grill for 10 to 15 minutes, with all the burners on high.

2. While the grill is preheating, melt the butter in a small saucepan over medium heat. Add the brown sugar and lime juice, and stir until dissolved and smooth. Keep the mixture warm.

3. Once the grill is hot, turn one burner off and turn the other(s) to medium. Position the bananas, skin side down, over the burner that is off, close the grill's lid, and cook for 5 to 8 minutes. Turn the bananas cut side down and grill them for an additional 2 minutes.

4. Transfer the bananas to a serving platter, remove the skins, and drizzle the warm sauce over the bananas. Serve immediately.

Serves 4

MAPLE-GLAZED PEACHES

Excellent eaten as is, right off the grill, peaches are ethereal when sliced over ice cream, especially if they're still warm!

4 fairly firm fresh peaches
2 tablespoons butter, melted
2 tablespoons pure maple syrup (or 2 tablespoons honey)

1. Preheat the grill for 10 to 15 minutes, with all the burners on high.

2. While the grill is preheating, cut the peaches in half, remove the pits, and brush the halves with melted butter.

3. Once the grill is hot, turn one burner off and turn the other(s) to medium. Position the peach halves, skin side up, over the burner that is off. Close the grill's lid and cook for 8 to 10 minutes, turning them once.

4. Serve warm, drizzled with a little real maple syrup.

Serves 4

If your grilling area lacks sufficient light, consider purchasing an old-fashioned kerosene lamp, which can generate a surprising amount of light and is very reliable.

GRILLED FRESH PINEAPPLE SPEARS

Grilled fresh pineapple is delicious on its own, as a dessert, or as a side dish to grilled ham. To tell if a pineapple is ripe, tug on one of the leaves: if it pulls out easily, the pineapple is at its peak and ready to grill.

1 fresh pineapple
4 tablespoons butter, melted

1. Preheat the grill for 10 to 15 minutes, with all the burners on high.

2. While the grill is preheating, cut the top and the bottom off the pineapple, then peel it. Cut the pineapple into quarters and remove the tough inner core. Slice each quarter into 1½-inch-thick wedges. Brush the pineapple with melted butter.

3. Once the grill is hot, turn one burner off and turn the other(s) to medium. Position the pineapple wedges over the burner that is off. Close the grill's lid and cook the pineapple for 10 to 12 minutes, turning it once. The pineapple will be done when it is lightly browned and heated through.

4. Serve hot off the grill.

Serves 4 to 6

•◆•

DESSERT BRUSCHETTA WITH CHEESE AND HONEY

•◆•

This unusual dessert was developed by Jay Harlow for *The Grilling Book*, which we co-authored in 1985. Upon first reading the ingredients, you may be put off, but by all means give it a try. The combination of flavors is outstanding!

1 loaf coarse-textured Italian or French bread
½ pound Pecorino Sardo, Asiago, fontina, or Gruyère
  cheese (listed in order of preference)
About ¼ cup extra-virgin olive oil
Honey, preferably with a strong flower or herb flavor

1. Preheat the grill for 10 to 15 minutes, with all the burners on high.

2. While the grill is preheating, slice the bread ¾ inch thick, and slice the cheese ¼ inch thick.

3. Once the grill is hot, turn one burner off and turn the other(s) to medium. Place the bread over the burner that is off and toast the pieces on one side. Turn the bread, drizzle olive oil generously on the toasted sides, and top each piece with a slice of cheese. Close the grill's lid and continue to cook the bread until the cheese melts (this should take only a couple of minutes).

4. As soon as the cheese has melted, transfer the bruschetta to a platter and drizzle with honey. Serve immediately.

Serves 6 to 8

•◆•

TOASTED POUND CAKE

•◆•

Sliced pound cake, lightly toasted on the grill, is a delightful end-of-the meal treat. You can make your own pound cake, of course, but the ones found in the frozen food section of your grocery store are quite good, too. Serve the grilled pound cake plain, or top with fresh berries, sliced peaches, or even ice cream.

9-inch loaf of pound cake
¼ cup butter, melted

1. Preheat the grill for 10 to 15 minutes, with all the burners on high.

2. While the grill is preheating, slice the pound cake into uniform slices, ¾ inch thick, and brush them lightly on both sides with melted butter.

3. Once the grill is hot, turn one burner off and turn the other(s) to medium. Place the slices of pound cake over the burner that is off. Close the grill's lid and cook the slices for 6 to 10 minutes, turning them once with a spatula.

4. Serve the cake hot off the grill, along with your favorite topping.

Serves 8

◆

OFF-THE-GRILL
SIDE DISHES

◆

CHAPTER NINE
OFF-THE-GRILL SIDE DISHES

The following recipes include a few vegetable dishes, but mostly they feature complex carbohydrates, such as potatoes, beans, and rice. Because grilled food is usually seasoned intensely, with either a marinade or other spice and herb mixtures, simple sides are best, so as not to overwhelm the diner with too many competing flavors.

Pasta is always welcome as a side dish, but again, keep it as simple as possible. Cooked pasta of any type can be moistened with olive oil, vegetable or chicken broth, or a sauce made from grilled tomatoes. You can add other ingredients—all types of vegetables, garlic, chopped fresh herbs, and, of course, fresh-grated Parmesan—according to a recipe or a whim. As a rule, omit meat (whether shellfish, sausage, or poultry) from pasta served as a side dish.

It's a fact of the kitchen that the simplest dishes, such as steamed rice or mashed potatoes, often require the most finesse—if only because there are so few ingredients with which to disguise a failure. With each of the following recipes, great care has been taken to give you all the information you need to ensure success, including detailed procedures and timing. It's good to remember, however, that the simplest of dishes rely more heavily than any others on the best possible ingredients.

++◆++

MARINATED VEGETABLE SALAD

++◆++

These crunchy vegetables make an excellent substitute for a green salad, particularly with grilled fish or a spicy dish that needs a little cooling off. The vegetables are best if they're made the night before you intend to serve them.

⅓ cup water
⅔ cup white vinegar
1 teaspoon salt
1 teaspoon celery seeds
½ teaspoon sugar
1 unwaxed European or English cucumber
2 carrots, cut in thin matchsticks
¼ cup chopped fresh dill, mint, or parsley

1. In a saucepan, combine the water, vinegar, salt, celery seeds, and sugar. Bring the mixture to a boil, cook the boiling liquid for 2 minutes, stirring it constantly, and remove the pan from the heat. Set the vinegar solution aside.

2. Score the cucumber lengthwise with a fork, repeating the action several times all the way around; the scores will give the individual cucumber slices a decorative pattern at the edges. Slice the cucumber thin, in ⅛-inch rounds, place the slices in a nonreactive bowl, and add the carrots.

3. Pour the warm vinegar solution over the cucumber and carrots. Add the dill, mint, or parsley and stir the vegetables. Cover the bowl and refrigerate for several hours, preferably overnight.

4. Serve the vegetables cold.

Serves 4 to 6

+·◆·+

NOT-YOUR-MOTHER'S
COLESLAW

+·◆·+

The cumin in this recipe, inspired by one from Julia Child, takes this coleslaw out of the ordinary. It pairs nicely with Cowpoke Beans (page 224) and any traditional barbecue fare, such as ribs or brisket.

3 cups grated green cabbage
3 cups grated purple cabbage
2 carrots, grated
1 red bell pepper, diced
6 green onions, minced
¼ cup chopped fresh parsley
⅔ cup plain yogurt
½ cup mayonnaise
Juice of ½ lemon
3 tablespoons white wine vinegar
1 tablespoon Dijon mustard
1 teaspoon ground cumin
Salt and fresh-ground black pepper to taste

1. In a large salad bowl, combine the cabbages, carrots, bell pepper, green onions, and parsley. Toss the ingredients to mix well.

2. In a small bowl, combine the yogurt, mayonnaise, lemon juice, vinegar, mustard, and cumin. Add the dressing to the vegetables and mix well. Season to taste with salt and pepper, and refrigerate the coleslaw for at least 1 hour.

3. Serve the coleslaw cold.

Serves 6 to 8

If there are kids in your household, make sure they understand that they shouldn't play around the grill. Never leave a hot grill unattended when there are children on the scene.

CREAMY RICE AND PEA SALAD

Rice and peas are a timeless combination, and this salad is a classic. For a while, rice salads seemed to be losing their place on the picnic table in favor of pasta salads. However, as rice and grains have become more fashionable, rice salads have made a remarkable comeback. This salad can be made with leftover cold rice, but it is better to combine all the ingredients while the rice is still hot and then refrigerate the salad.

1⅓ cups uncooked white rice
2⅔ cups water
1 teaspoon salt
½ cup mayonnaise
2 tablespoons Dijon mustard
¼ cup extra-virgin olive oil
2 tablespoons red or white wine vinegar
1 tablespoon curry powder (optional)
10-ounce package frozen peas (preferably baby or "petits pois"), thawed
⅓ cup minced green onions
Salt and fresh-ground black pepper to taste

1. Rinse the rice in several changes of cold water until the water runs clear. Drain well.

2. Combine the rice, water, and salt in a medium saucepan.

Cover the pan and bring the water to a boil. Reduce the heat and simmer the rice until it is tender and the water is absorbed, 15 to 20 minutes.

3. While the rice is cooking, in a small bowl, mix together the mayonnaise, mustard, olive oil, vinegar, and curry powder, if desired. Set the dressing aside.

4. When the rice is done, spoon it into a large salad bowl. Add the mayonnaise dressing and mix well. Season the mixture to taste with salt and pepper. If the rice seems a little dry, add a bit more olive oil.

5. Gently fold the peas and onions into the rice mixture. Refrigerate the salad in the bowl for several hours. Alternatively, to form a salad mold, lightly oil another bowl, press the rice salad into it, and refrigerate for at least 2 hours.

6. Serve the cold salad straight from the bowl, or if you molded it, turn it out upside-down onto a bed of lettuce before serving.

Serves 6 to 8

•✦•

SAUTÉED LETTUCE WITH PEAS

•✦•

Even people who supposedly hate peas like them prepared in this traditional French manner. Just don't overcook the peas; they should still be bright green when served. If you can find them, buy baby peas, sometimes labeled "petits pois."

2 tablespoons butter
2 cups shredded iceberg lettuce
10-ounce package frozen baby green peas
2 tablespoons minced fresh parsley
½ teaspoon sugar
Dash of ground nutmeg
Salt to taste

1. Melt the butter in a large frying pan over medium-high heat. Add the lettuce while the butter is still bubbling, and sauté for 1 to 2 minutes. Mix in the frozen peas, parsley, sugar, nutmeg, and salt. Reduce the heat to medium, cover the pan, and cook the vegetables for 6 to 8 minutes, just until the peas are tender and heated through.

2. Serve immediately.

Serves 4

+·◆·+

CREAMED SPINACH

·◆·+

This old-fashioned dish is still popular with discerning diners. I particularly like it with grilled fish.

2 pounds fresh spinach
2 tablespoons butter
2 tablespoons all-purpose flour
1 cup half-and-half (or light cream)
½ teaspoon dry mustard
⅛ teaspoon ground nutmeg
Salt and fresh-ground black pepper to taste

1. Wash the spinach in several changes of cold water and drain well. Remove the stems from the spinach. Add about 1 inch of water to a large pot, place the leaves inside, and steam the spinach for 3 to 5 minutes, or until the leaves are limp. Drain the spinach well, grabbing handfuls of it and squeezing out the excess water. Chop the leaves, drain the spinach again, and reserve.

2. Melt the butter in a heavy-bottomed saucepan over medium heat. Add the flour, 1 tablespoon at a time, stirring constantly with a wooden spoon or wire whisk. Cook the mixture for 2 to 3 minutes, but do not let it brown. Add the half-and-half, and continue to stir the sauce while it boils and then thickens. Increase the heat slightly, if necessary. Mix in the dry mustard, nutmeg, and salt and pepper.

3. Add the chopped spinach to the cream sauce, mix well, and adjust the seasonings.

4. Serve the spinach immediately.

Serves 4 to 6

⁺◆⁺ TEX-MEX BLACK-EYED PEAS ⁺◆⁺

There is something about the characteristic flavor of black-eyed peas that complements most grilled foods, particularly those with a Southwestern or Mexican accent.

1 tablespoon vegetable oil
1 small onion, minced
2 garlic cloves, pressed
10-ounce package fresh or frozen black-eyed peas
½ cup chicken stock
2 teaspoons chili powder
1 teaspoon ground cumin
Salt and fresh-ground black pepper to taste
Chopped fresh parsley, for garnish (optional)

1. Warm the oil in a medium saucepan over medium-high heat. Add the onion and garlic, and sauté until the onion is soft but not brown, about 4 minutes.

2. Add the fresh or frozen black-eyed peas, chicken stock, chili powder, and cumin to the pan and mix well. Continue to cook vegetables over medium heat until the peas are just tender, about 15 minutes. Add salt and pepper to taste.

3. Serve the peas hot, garnished with parsley if desired.

Serves 4

⁺◆⁺ COWPOKE BEANS ⁺◆⁺

Beans go well with most grilled meats, but they have a special affinity for red meats. Add some cornbread and coleslaw and you have a great-tasting, rustic meal—the kind that tastes best eaten out-of-doors.

½ pound sliced bacon
2 medium yellow onions, minced
3 garlic cloves, pressed

Three 15-ounce cans pinto beans, rinsed and drained
12 ounces beer
1 cup chicken or beef stock
28-ounce can whole peeled tomatoes, undrained
2 to 3 tablespoons chili powder
1 tablespoon ground cumin
1 teaspoon dried oregano leaves
Salt and fresh-ground black pepper to taste

1. Cook the bacon in a Dutch oven until crisp. Remove the bacon strips and drain them on paper towels. Crumble the bacon and set aside.

2. Drain off all but 2 tablespoons of the bacon grease in the Dutch oven. Add the onions and garlic, and sauté until the onions are soft but not brown, about 4 minutes.

3. Add the remaining ingredients to the pot, stir the mixture, and bring it to a boil. Reduce the heat to low and simmer the beans, uncovered, for about 30 minutes.

4. Serve the beans hot, with the crumbled bacon sprinkled on top.

Serves 6 to 8

•◦◆◦•

BAKED HOMINY CUSTARD

•◦◆◦•

This custard is delicious paired with grilled pork or ham.

4 tablespoons butter
¼ cup all-purpose flour
1 cup scalded milk (hot, but not boiling)
Pinch of cayenne, or 2 shakes of Tabasco sauce
1 cup grated cheddar cheese
15½-ounce can hominy, drained
1 red bell pepper, diced
4-ounce can chopped green chiles
4 eggs
Butter and cornmeal

1. Preheat the oven to 375° F.

2. While the oven is preheating, melt the butter in a heavy-bottomed saucepan over medium-high heat. Using a wooden spoon or wire whisk, stir in the flour and blend until smooth, about 2 or 3 minutes.

3. Slowly add the hot milk to the butter-flour mixture, stirring constantly. Continue to stir for 2 to 3 minutes until the mixture is thick and smooth. Add the cayenne or Tabasco, cheese, hominy, red pepper, and green chiles. Stir the mixture until the cheese has melted.

4. Remove the pan from the heat and allow the mixture to cool for about 5 minutes. While it's cooling, beat the eggs. Spoon about ¼ cup of the cooled hominy mixture into the beaten eggs. Stir the eggs and hominy, pour them into the saucepan, and mix well.

5. Grease a 2-quart baking dish generously with butter or margarine and dust it with cornmeal. Pour the hominy mixture into the dish and bake for 40 to 45 minutes, until the custard has set.

6. Serve the custard hot out of the oven.

Serves 4

⋅⋅◆⋅⋅
BOILED NEW POTATOES
⋅⋅◆⋅⋅

Tender, boiled new potatoes, served with nothing more than a little butter and chopped dill, can be found in just about every grill restaurant in this country and in Europe. The little ones (about the size of a pullet egg) are considered first choice; the larger new potatoes may not be quite as attractive on a plate, but they're still great eating.

> *About 20 new potatoes*
> *Salt*
> *3 to 6 tablespoons butter*
> *¼ cup chopped fresh dill*

1. Wash and scrub the new potatoes under cold water, but do not peel them. Put the potatoes in a pot, cover with about 2 inches

Spiders, attracted to the smell of an additive used in gas, sometimes get lodged in a grill's tubing. If you're having trouble lighting your grill, spiders could well be the problem. Consult your owner's manual to learn how to clean out the tubes.

of water, and sprinkle in some salt. Cover the pot and bring the water to a boil. Cook the potatoes until a sharp knife easily pierces their center. The cooking time depends on the size of the potatoes: 3-inch potatoes will take 20 to 25 minutes.

2. Drain the potatoes, toss them with the butter and dill, and serve hot.

Serves 4

HOMEMADE FRENCH FRIES

French-fried potatoes, or *pommes frites*, as the French call them, are delicious with almost any grilled fare—especially steaks, chops, and fish. Double-frying is the secret to achieving the best results.

4 large, brown-skinned baking potatoes (about 1 per person)
4 cups vegetable oil, preferably peanut
Salt and fresh-ground black pepper to taste

1. Wash and scrub the potatoes in cold water, but do not peel them. Using a sharp knife or a food processor, cut the potatoes into uniform, ⅜-inch-square sticks about 3 to 4 inches long.

2. In a deep, heavy pan, heat the oil to 300° F. Add the potatoes to the oil, in about 3 batches, and fry each batch for 4 to 5 minutes. Use a long-handled fork to keep the potatoes from sticking together as they cook. The goal is to partially cook or soften the potatoes, not brown them. While the potatoes cook, line a cookie sheet with several layers of paper towels.

3. With a slotted spoon, transfer the potatoes to the cookie sheet and let them drain. If you will be serving the potatoes later the same day, let them sit at room temperature, for up to 4 hours. Otherwise, cover them loosely and refrigerate overnight.

4. A few minutes before serving time, reheat the oil—this time to 375° F. Divide the partially cooked fries into 3 batches and fry them for about 3 minutes, or until they turn a light golden brown.

Remove the potatoes from the oil with a slotted spoon and drain them on clean paper towels.

5. Transfer the french fries to a basket, sprinkle them with salt and pepper, and serve.

Serves 4

••◆••
POTATO TART
••◆••

F rench in origin, this potato tart represents rustic, farm-house cooking at its best. Serve it with any grilled meat.

4 large baking potatoes
3 tablespoons olive oil
5 tablespoons butter
4 garlic cloves, pressed
4 tablespoons chopped fresh tarragon, or 1 tablespoon
*   dried tarragon*
Salt and fresh-ground black pepper to taste
Chopped fresh parsley, for garnish (optional)

1. Wash and peel the potatoes, then slice them into ³⁄₁₆-inch rounds, as evenly as possible. Put the potatoes in a bowl of cold water until you're ready for the next step (or they will turn brown).

2. Heat the oil and 2 tablespoons of the butter in a large, heavy skillet with a lid. Add the garlic and cook for 30 seconds. Remove the pan from the heat.

3. Drain the potato slices on paper towels and blot them dry. Chop 2 more tablespoons of butter into small bits. Add the potato slices to the pan, arranging them in layers of overlapping, concentric circles. Sprinkle each layer with a little of the tarragon, chopped butter, and salt and pepper. When all the potatoes have been arranged in the pan, press them down firmly with a lid or plate so that they hold together a bit.

4. Cover the skillet and cook the potatoes over medium heat for 5 minutes. Remove the lid and continue cooking for 15 minutes or so; lower the heat if you think the potatoes on the bottom are about to burn.

5. Loosen the potatoes with a spatula or a knife, so that they will flip out of the skillet more easily. Cover the skillet with a large inverted plate (one that's larger than the skillet by a couple of inches), hold the plate in place with one hand, and carefully turn the skillet upside-down. Add the remaining tablespoon of butter to the skillet and ease the potatoes, brown side up, back into the pan. Cook the potatoes for another 15 minutes over medium heat, to brown the other side of the tart.

6. Using the same method as in step 5, flip the potato tart onto an inverted serving plate, sprinkle with parsley, if desired, and serve immediately.

Serves 4

···◆···

SAUERKRAUT-AND-POTATO CASSEROLE

···◆···

This is a hearty side dish, great with any type of grilled pork, ham, or sausages. If you want to make the dish less salty, rinse the sauerkraut after draining it.

*3 or 4 large baking potatoes, washed, peeled, and sliced ½
  inch thick*
4 bacon slices
1 onion, sliced thin
2 pounds sauerkraut, drained and rinsed
2 carrots, sliced 1 inch thick
¾ cup beer, chicken stock, or a mixture of the two
1 teaspoon caraway seeds
Fresh-ground black pepper to taste

1. Boil the potato slices in salted water until they are tender, about 10 minutes. Drain the potatoes well.

2. In a large skillet or Dutch oven, cook the bacon until crisp. With a slotted spoon, transfer the bacon to paper towels and drain well. Discard all but 1 tablespoon of the bacon grease from the pan.

3. Add the onion slices to the pan and sauté over medium heat until soft, about 3 minutes. Add the potato slices, sauerkraut, carrots, beer or chicken stock (or a combination of the two), caraway seeds, and pepper. Toss the mixture lightly.

4. Cover the pan and cook the vegetables over medium heat until the carrots are tender, about 15 minutes.

5. Spoon the mixture into a serving dish, crumble the bacon over the top, and serve.

Serves 4 to 6

RISOTTO

What makes Italian risotto so creamy, tender, and delicious is the rice itself. Risotto must be made with a unique, almost round, short-grain rice from Italy. The only rice commonly available in this country for making risotto is Arborio; in Italy they have a choice of Arborio, Canaroli, Nano, or Vialone. The secret of these plump little grains is that they contain sufficient starch to absorb large quantities of liquid, which in turn results in risotto's characteristic creaminess. Although risotto is at its best when served immediately, it can be kept warm in the top of a double boiler—over hot but not boiling water—for about 1 hour.

Note: You may not need the entire amount of broth indicated; it all depends on the degree of heat at which you're cooking the risotto. Risotto that is partially covered halfway through the cooking time will absorb much less stock (sometimes no more than 2 to 3 cups).

> *2 tablespoons extra-virgin olive oil*
> *2 shallots, minced*
> *1 cup Arborio rice*
> *⅓ cup dry white wine*
> *4 to 5 cups hot chicken broth*
> *Salt and fresh-ground black pepper to taste*
> *2 tablespoons butter (optional)*
> *3 to 4 tablespoons Parmesan cheese (optional)*
> *Chopped fresh parsley, for garnish (optional)*

Get in the habit of putting serving plates in a 200° F oven for 10 minutes before serving time. Hot food on hot plates is a simple luxury anyone can afford.

1. Warm the olive oil in a large, heavy-bottomed skillet or saucepan over low heat. Add the shallots and sauté until very soft but not brown, 3 to 4 minutes.

2. Add the rice to the pan and blend it with the shallots. Stir in the wine, raise the heat to medium-high, and cook the mixture until the wine has completely evaporated.

3. Start adding the broth ½ cup at a time, stirring the rice constantly. Keep the heat moderately high so that the rice absorbs the liquid but does not dry out too quickly. Continue adding the broth ½ cup at a time as the liquid is absorbed.

4. After about 20 minutes, start adding the broth ¼ cup at a time. If the rice is still partly chewy, cover the pan partially and let the rice cook a little more slowly, allowing it to absorb the liquid. Keep an eye on it. The finished rice will be a creamy mass with kernels that are soft but still chewy.

5. When the rice is done, adjust the seasoning carefully with salt and pepper. Add the butter, if desired, stir well, and cook the rice another 2 to 3 minutes, or until the butter is well absorbed. If you wish, stir in the Parmesan cheese.

6. Transfer the rice to a hot serving dish, sprinkle it with parsley if you like, and serve.

Serves 4 to 6

•◆•

BASMATI RICE CAKE

•◆•

With extra-long grains, a flowery, buttery aroma, and superior flavor and texture, basmati rice is well worth its premium price. Delicious when simply boiled or steamed, basmati rice is even better when prepared as follows.

1 cup basmati rice
1 teaspoon salt
2 tablespoons extra-virgin olive oil
Several saffron threads, pulverized between your thumb
  and forefinger
¼ cup chopped green onions or fresh chives

1. Place the rice in a strainer and rinse it in several changes of cold water, until the water runs clear. Drain the rice well.

2. Transfer the rice to a saucepan, add the salt, and add enough water to cover the rice with 1 inch of water.

3. Bring the rice to a boil over medium-high heat. Immediately lower the heat and simmer the rice, uncovered, until soft—about 15 to 20 minutes. Test the rice by biting into a grain: it should not be chalky.

4. Drain the rice, rinse it with cold water, and set it aside.

5. Coat the bottom and sides of a heavy skillet with the oil (a well-seasoned cast iron or heavy nonstick skillet works well), and warm over medium heat. Once the skillet is warm, add the rice and mix in the saffron and green onions or chives. Cover the skillet with a clean towel, and cover the towel with a lid or a large plate. Reduce the heat to low and cook the rice for 20 to 25 minutes.

6. Remove the lid and the towel from the pan. Using a flexible spatula or knife, loosen the rice from the edges of the skillet. Cover the skillet with a large, inverted serving plate (one that is an inch or so larger than the skillet) and, holding the plate in place with one hand, turn the skillet upside-down. Serve immediately.

Serves 4

⁺⁺◆⁺⁺

WILD RICE CASSEROLE

⁺⁺◆⁺⁺

This casserole is excellent as an accompaniment to hearty grilled fare such as roasts and game. People who know wild rice well almost always cook it in chicken stock rather than water.

Butter
2 tablespoons olive oil
½ cup chopped onion
2 cups sliced mushrooms
1 cup wild rice
3 cups chicken stock
Salt and fresh-ground black pepper to taste

1. Preheat the oven to 350° F. Butter the bottom and sides of a 1½-quart oven-proof casserole dish.

2. Warm the oil in a large skillet over medium-high heat. Add the onion and mushrooms and sauté until soft. Spoon the sautéed mushrooms and onions into the casserole dish, and add the remaining ingredients. Cover the dish and bake the rice for 1 hour, or until all the liquid has been absorbed and the rice is tender.

3. Serve hot out of the oven.

Serves 4

•◆•
POLENTA
•◆•

Polenta—an Italian version of our cornmeal mush—is a simple and satisfying side dish. To make authentic polenta, you'll need the proper ingredients; regular cornmeal won't do because it is ground too fine. It's the coarser cornmeal, specially ground for polenta, that you want. In some Italian groceries, you'll find "Instant Polenta," which cooks up in a matter of minutes. It's more expensive than regular polenta but certainly a lot easier to make—and every bit as good.

7 cups water
1 tablespoon salt
2 cups coarse-ground, polenta cornmeal
4 tablespoons butter, cut into pats
½ cup grated Parmesan cheese

1. Pour the water and the salt into a large pot—one with a handle you can grip comfortably. (You're going to be gripping it for about 20 minutes, so you might as well be comfortable.) Bring the water to a boil over high heat.

2. Reduce the heat so that the water is at a low boil. Add the cornmeal, one handful at a time, letting it slowly sift through your fingers. Keep stirring, stirring, stirring, adding the cornmeal one handful at a time, until it is used up.

3. Stir the polenta until it starts to pull away from the sides of the pot. Add the butter and parmesan cheese and stir until blended.

4. Transfer the polenta to a pre-warmed platter, and serve it forth.

Serves 6 to 8

INDEX